COFFEE TABLE BOOK OF PRIDE FLAGS

Coffee Table Book of Pride Flags

Discovering the LGBT+ Community Through Art

JENNIFER FREDERICK

First Printing, 2026

Contents

To all of the people who have wondered if there's something wrong with them, felt out of place, or just wanted to find a word that described their experiences, this is for you.

You're not alone.

Chapter 1

Introduction

What You Need to Know Before Reading

Terminology, a few notes, and some pride flags to get you started before you really dive in!

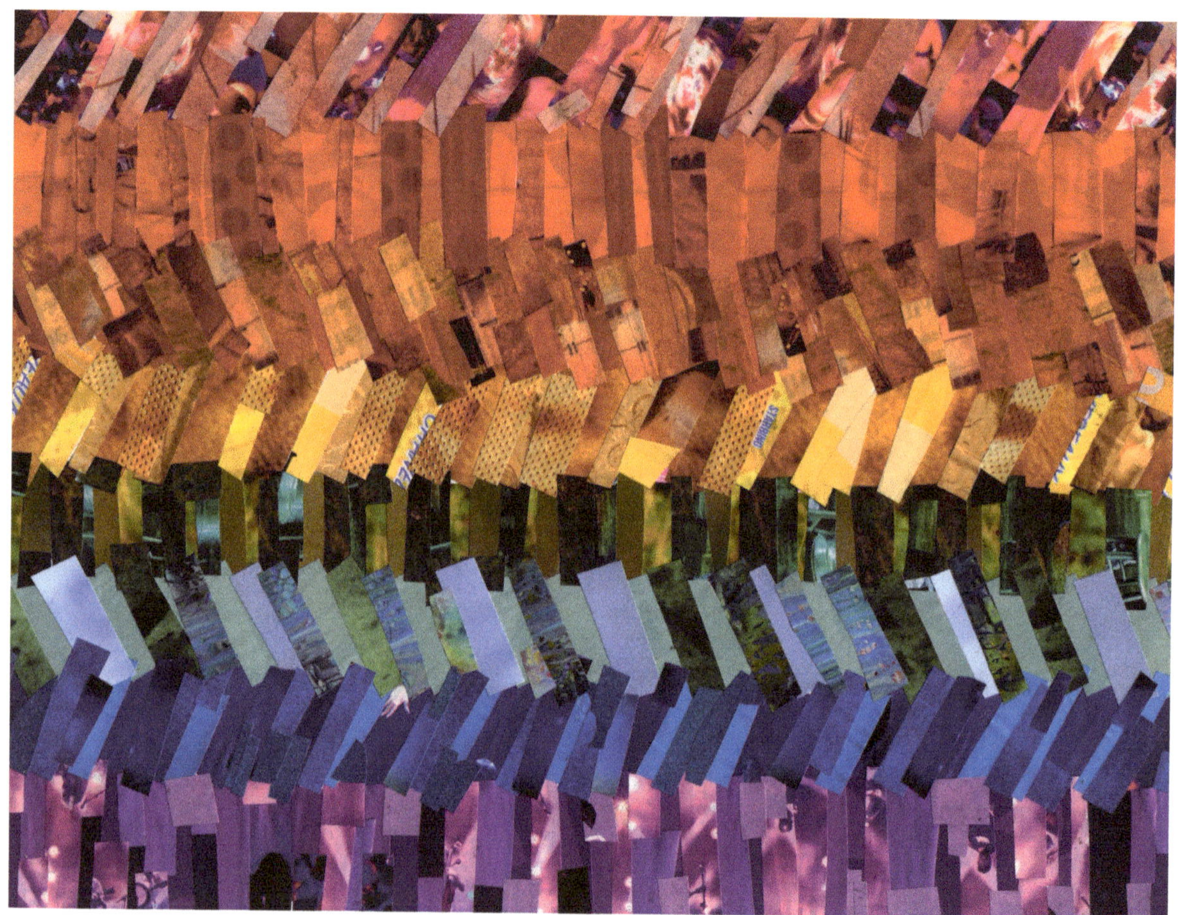

Gilbert Baker Pride Flag: The original pride flag designed in 1978. Pink stands for sex, red for life, orange for healing, yellow for sunlight, green for nature, turquoise for magic/art, blue for serenity, and purple for spirit.

A Quick Note for Readers

Please keep in mind that definitions provided here-in are often rather squishy and not as rigid as any wording may suggest. Identity is something that intensely personal and comes down to each person alone.

On top of this, many people experience split attraction where their romantic orientation may not be the same as their sexual orientation. This is merely meant to be an intro to some of the many orientations that make up the vibrant and diverse community we have today.

Not every orientation has one set flag, and flags have changed over time. Those included in here are artistic renditions by the author to represent some of them.

All language in this book is meant to be inclusive and mostly avoids gendered pronouns except in very specific sections.

This book is not meant to be a comprehensive look at pride flags, rather a very broad one. Language constantly evolves and new labels are made, so if something it is not listed here, it is one I was not aware of. I hope it provides some insight into the LGBT+ identities that you might not have otherwise had knowledge of while providing artistic interpretation of the pride flags.

With over 5% (and often growing) of the United States currently identifying as LGBT+,[1] these all mean very different things to each person. Each meaning is just as valid, and many people will cycle through at least some of these identities in their lifetime as gender and orientation tend to be fluid for everyone as they gain insight into who they are.

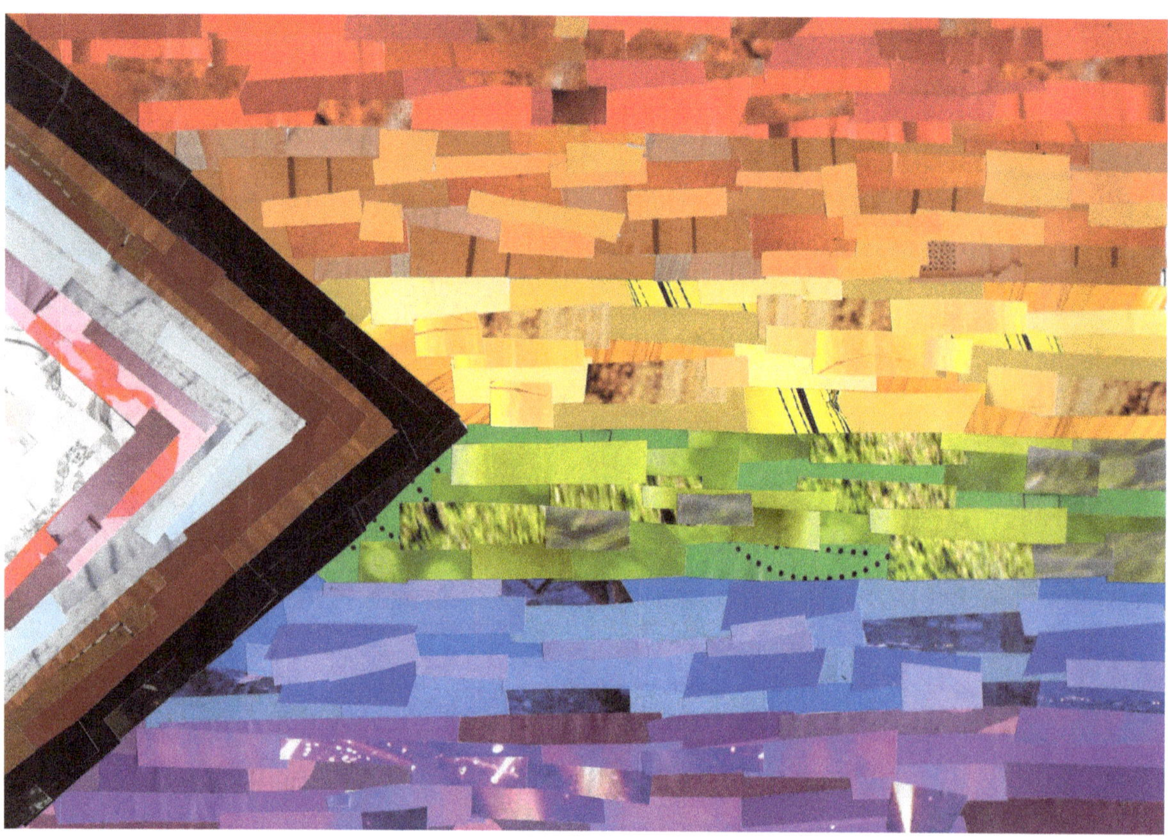

The Progress Pride Flag: This pride flag was made to build upon the Philadelphia Pride Flag by including not only black and brown stripes for people of color but also a light blue, light pink, and white chevron to represent the trans community and their struggles. The chevrons on the side are meant to incorporate these stripes even more than just tacking them on to the beginning or end of the rainbow to show better inclusion.

On Terminology

This book addresses the LGBT+ community. While most of the terminology is going to be introduced with each flag, there are a few terms that should be noted beforehand. Below, some terms are listed to help you navigate this book and how I am defining these terms.

Romantic Orientation: How someone experiences romantic attraction.

Sexual Orientation: How someone experiences sexual attraction.

Platonic Attraction: The attraction of wishing to be close to someone emotionally, can be more intense than just wishing to be friends.

Sensual Attraction: a desire for input or output like holding hands, being physically close to someone.

Aesthetic Attraction: appreciating someone's appearance without having romantic or sexual attraction attached to it.

Alterous Attraction: when you want to be emotionally close to someone but do not want it to be just romantic or platonic but rather something in between.

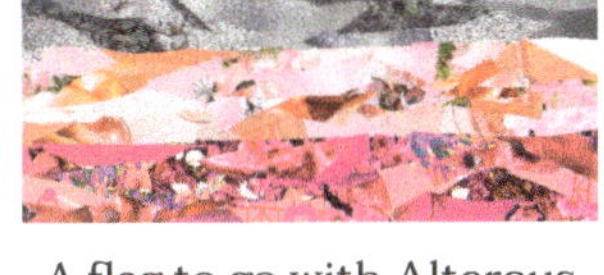

A flag to go with Alterous attraction.

Heterosexual: Being sexually attracted to only a different gender.

Heteroromantic: Being romantically attracted to only a different gender.

Cisgender: Identifying with the gender one was assigned at birth.

Allosexual/Alloromantic: People who experience sexual or romantic attraction.

Gender Presentation: What someone looks like to other people. This may not line up with someone's gender identity.

Gender Identity: The actual gender one identifies with. This may not line up with gender presentation.

Microlabel: A label someone uses that could fall under a broader umbrella of or overlaps with another identity.

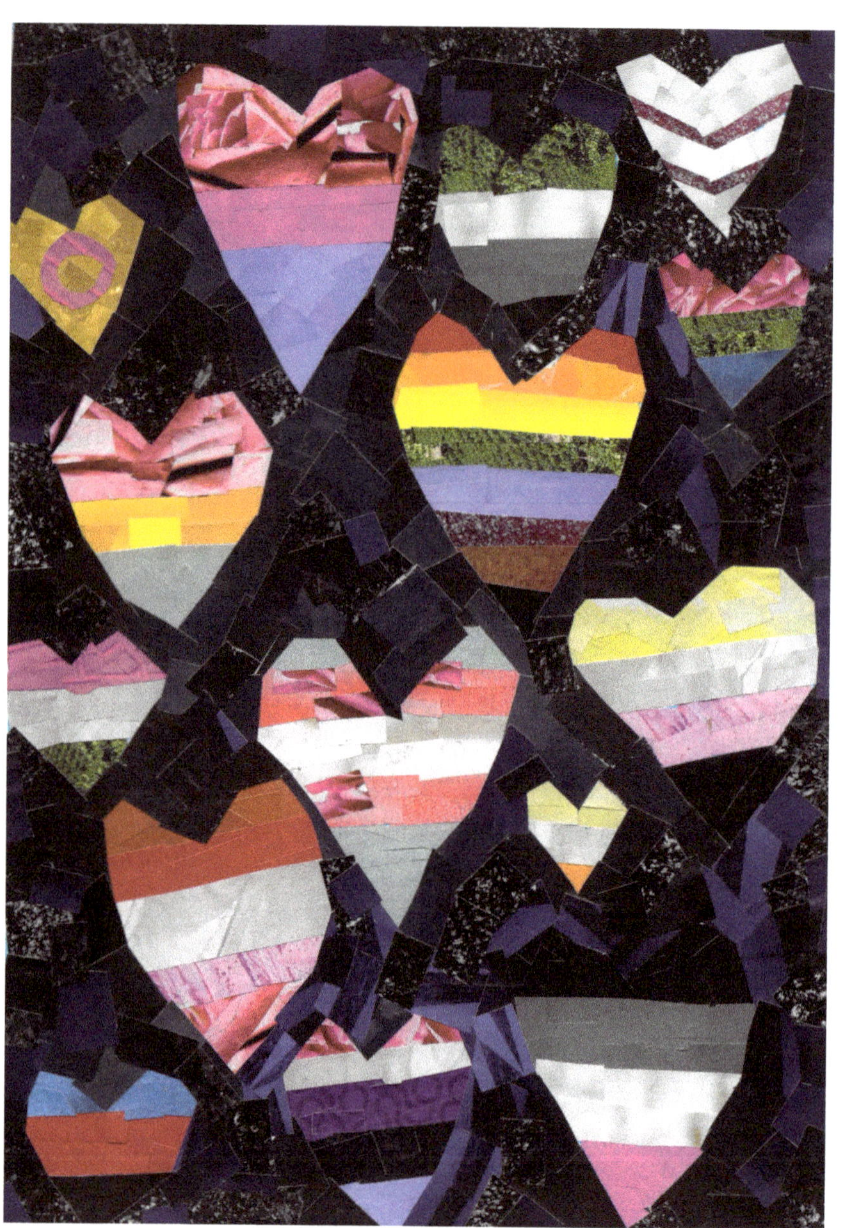

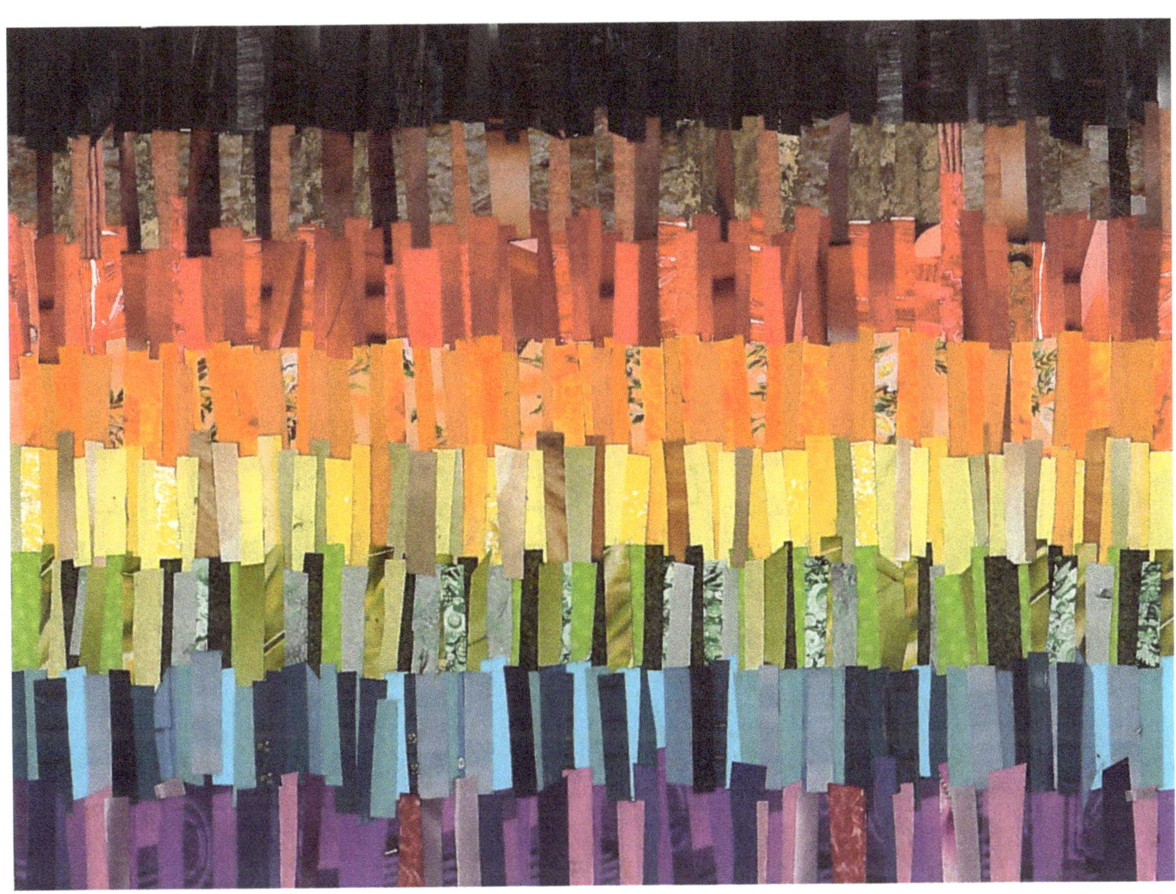

Philadelphia Pride Flag: Made in 2017 to represent the struggles that black and brown LGBT+ people go through as part of the community and how their struggles take place with and alongside the LGBT+ community.

What is it to be LGBT+? Or LGBTQIA? Or Queer?

There are many umbrella terms for what it means to be an LGBT+ person. However, the basics are recognized as someone who does not identify as a heterosexual, heteroromantic, and cisgender individual.

People have differed on what to call themselves as a community, especially with many of the community's identifiers being seeped with hatred or used as a slur at some point in time. However, there is still much pride around being part of the LGBT+ community, and many find their home among it.

As time has gone on, we have gained a number of pride flags, variations on the traditional rainbow and others. These recognize individuals lived experience being different but still part of our community. From Gilbert Baker's original rainbow of eight stripes to the Philadelphia Pride flag that recognizes how black and brown people experience homophobia, transphobia, and racism in a way that cannot be separated, our flags help represent us and bring pride.

This book is dedicated to those pride flags and the many identities that can fall under the umbrella of our community. The first few will be in order of the acronym before moving into less well-known identities.

Chapter 2

Well Known LGBT+ Identities

This section will cover the pride flags you are the most likely to already know and may recognize. If this is your first intro to them, then welcome!

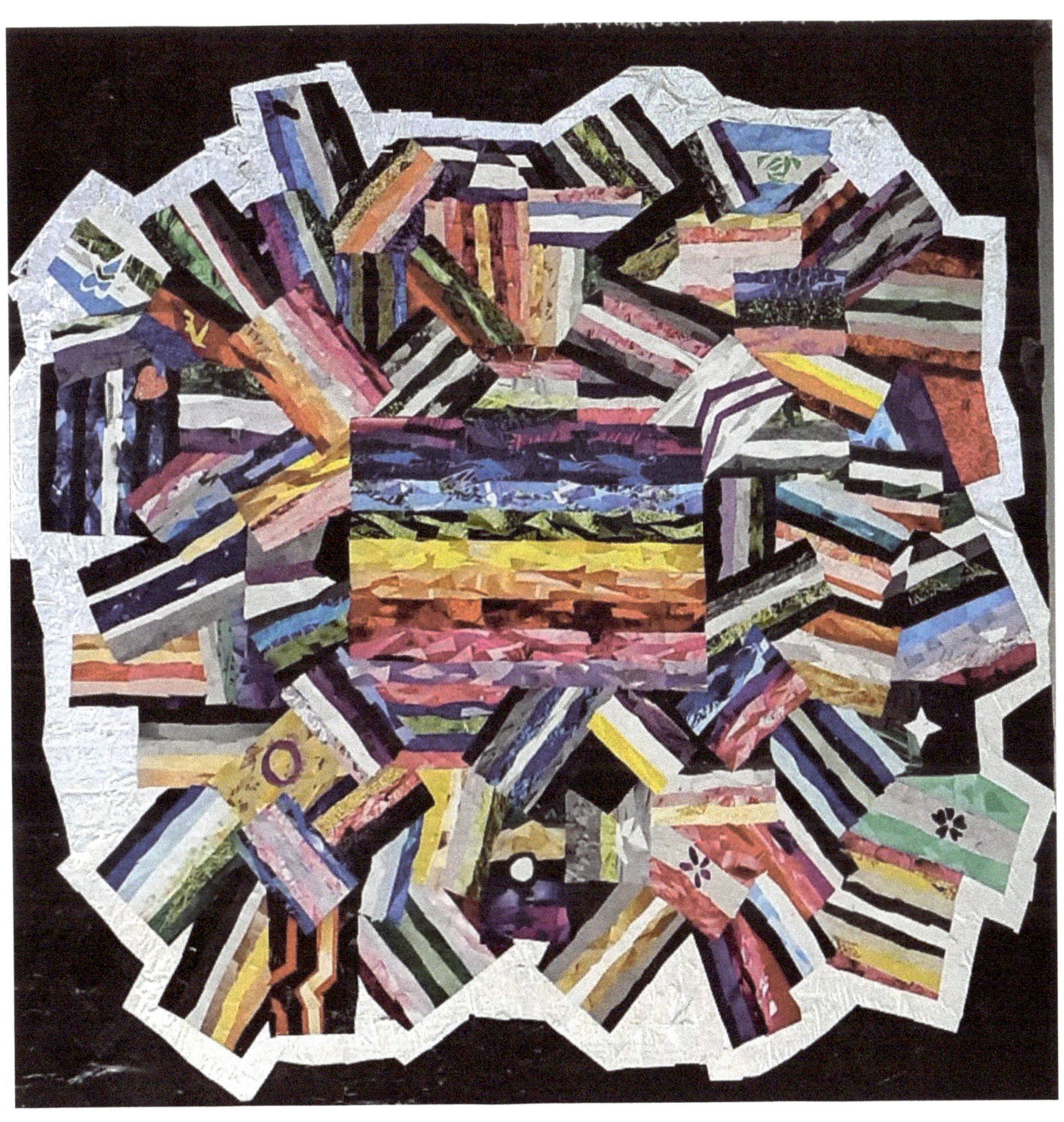

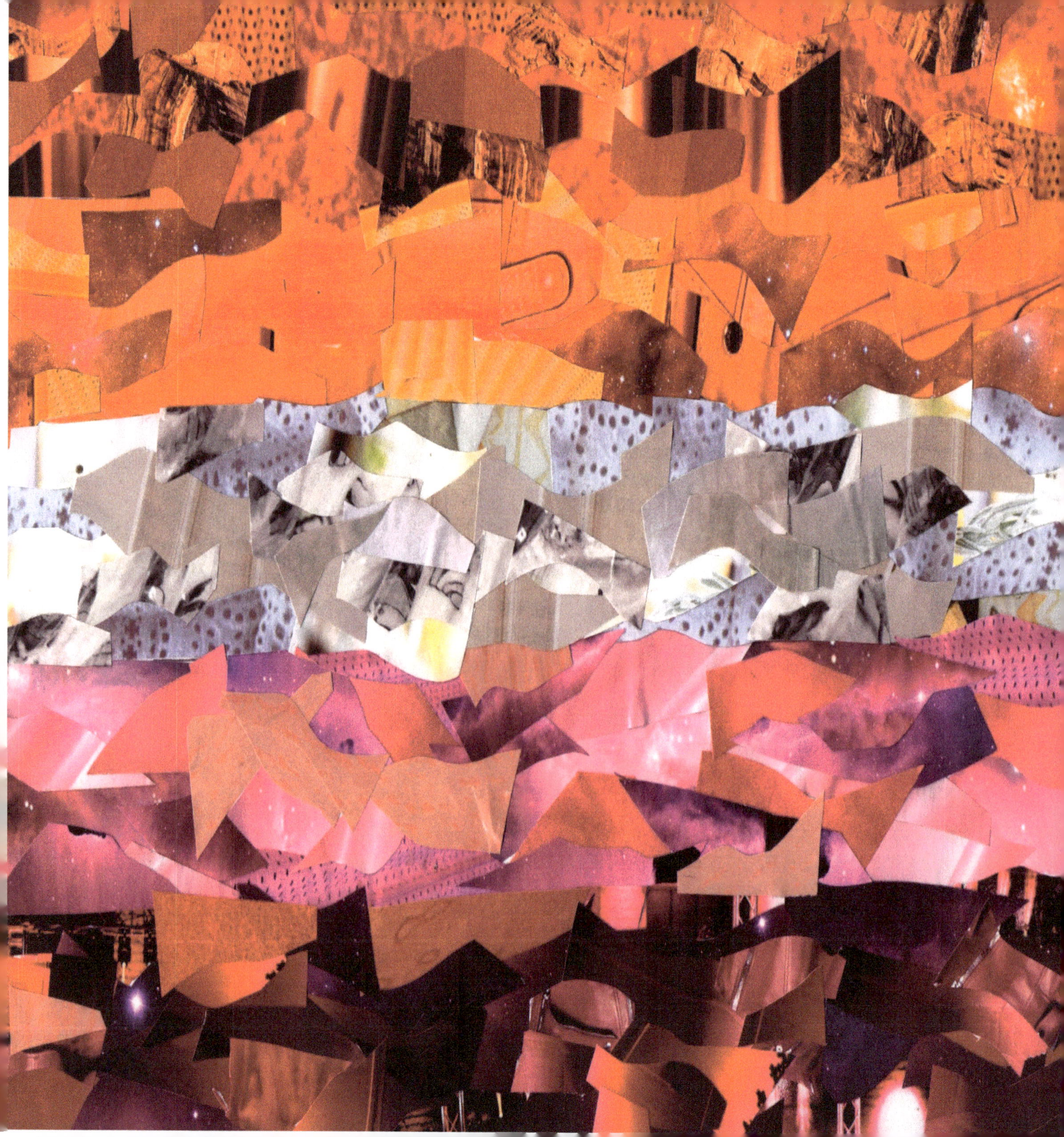

Lesbian

Lesbian is often the first identity listed off when talking about the LGBT+ community, though it hasn't always been this way. Before the current acronym, sometimes the community was called GLBT or other variations with Gay coming first. The L began to come first after the AIDs crisis in recognition of how lesbians stepped in to take care of those affected by the pandemic that killed many in the community.

Typically, lesbian is defined as a woman who is romantically and sexually attracted to women. However, there is some grey area here as plenty of nonbinary people identify as lesbian.

Also, plenty of gay women do not identify as lesbian. Whether it is because the word gay suits them better or for another reason, this is not the term for every woman attracted to women.

Pictured on the left are the sunset lesbian pride flags. There is also a lipstick lesbian flag which is generally considered more out of date as it was made strictly for femme lesbians and then was used more broadly for all lesbians. Still, both are broadly used.

The sunset lesbian flag is a gradient from orange to dark pink in five stripes. The lipstick lesbian flag is a gradient of seven stripes from pink to red.

Well Known Lesbians: Megan Rapinoe (USWNT Soccer Player), Audre Lorde (author and poet), and Hayley Kiyoko (singer).

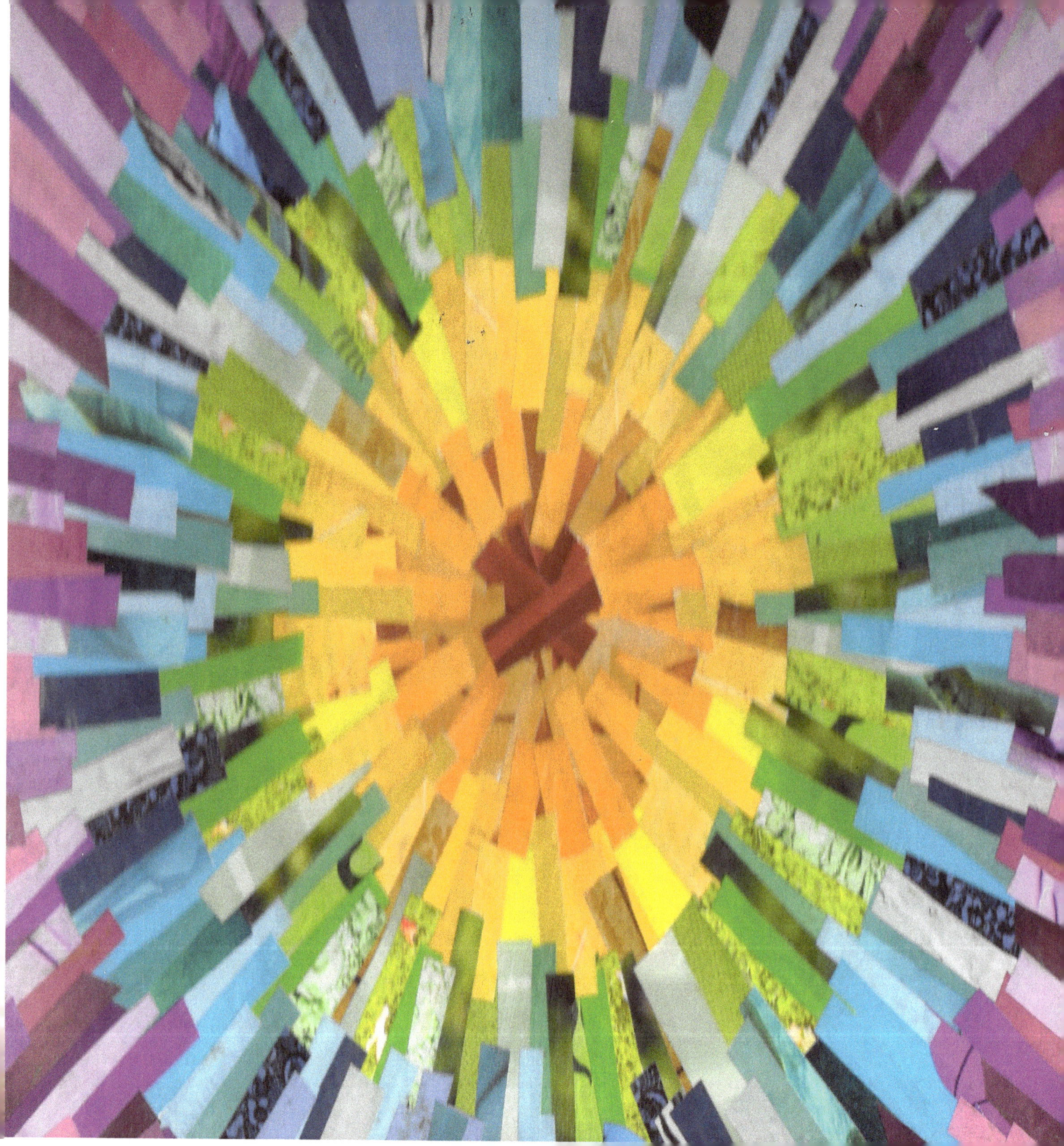

Gay

Probably the most well known of any identity, gay is used by people who are attracted to the same gender. Often, gay men are the most common people to use this description. Still, many women use it as well as mentioned before.

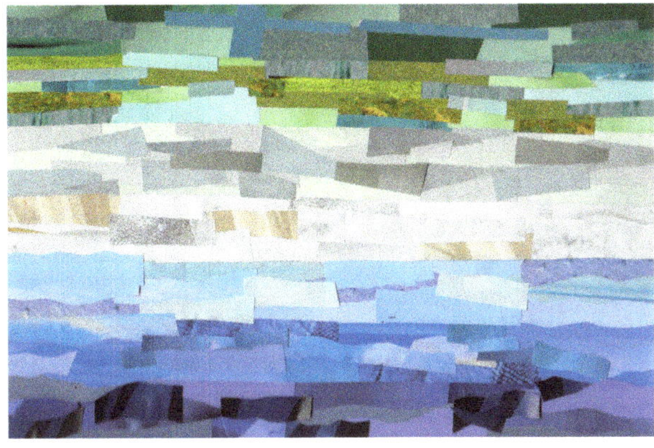

Gay is also used as a term to describe the whole community of LGBT+ people on occasion. The gay community does not mean that a person is necessarily part of people attracted to the same people, just that they don't identify as cisgender, heteroromantic, and heterosexual.

Today, the gay flag is generally the same as the rainbow flag for the whole community.

There has been a movement behind the blue and green flag of five stripes for gay men specifically that want a more specific flag like other groups though! This one is not as popular but has gained some traction in recent years.

Well Known Gays: Elton John (singer and song writer), Alan Turing (broke the Enigma Code in WWII), Officer Francois Clemmons (on Mr. Roger's Neighborhood), and Ron Oden (first black , openly gay man to be mayor of a US city).

Bi

Bisexual and Biromantic people are attracted to more than one gender. They are probably the most well-known multi-gender attracted group of people.

Bi people are just as much part of the community. Being attracted to a different gender is not grounds for exclusion from the LGBT+ community, but they often face biphobia from lesbian, gay, and heterosexual people. This can be through erasure of their identity, refusing to recognize they are just as good a partner as a person who is attracted to a single gender, and saying that they will 'eventually pick aside'.

Still, they have been and continue to be an incredible part of the LGBT+ community.

Their flag is pink and blue with a thin purple stripe in the middle, representing attraction to different genders through these colors.

Well Known Bis: Lady Gaga (singer/song writer), Chloe Auli'i Cravalho (Actress and voice of Moana), and David Bowie (singer, song writer, and actor).

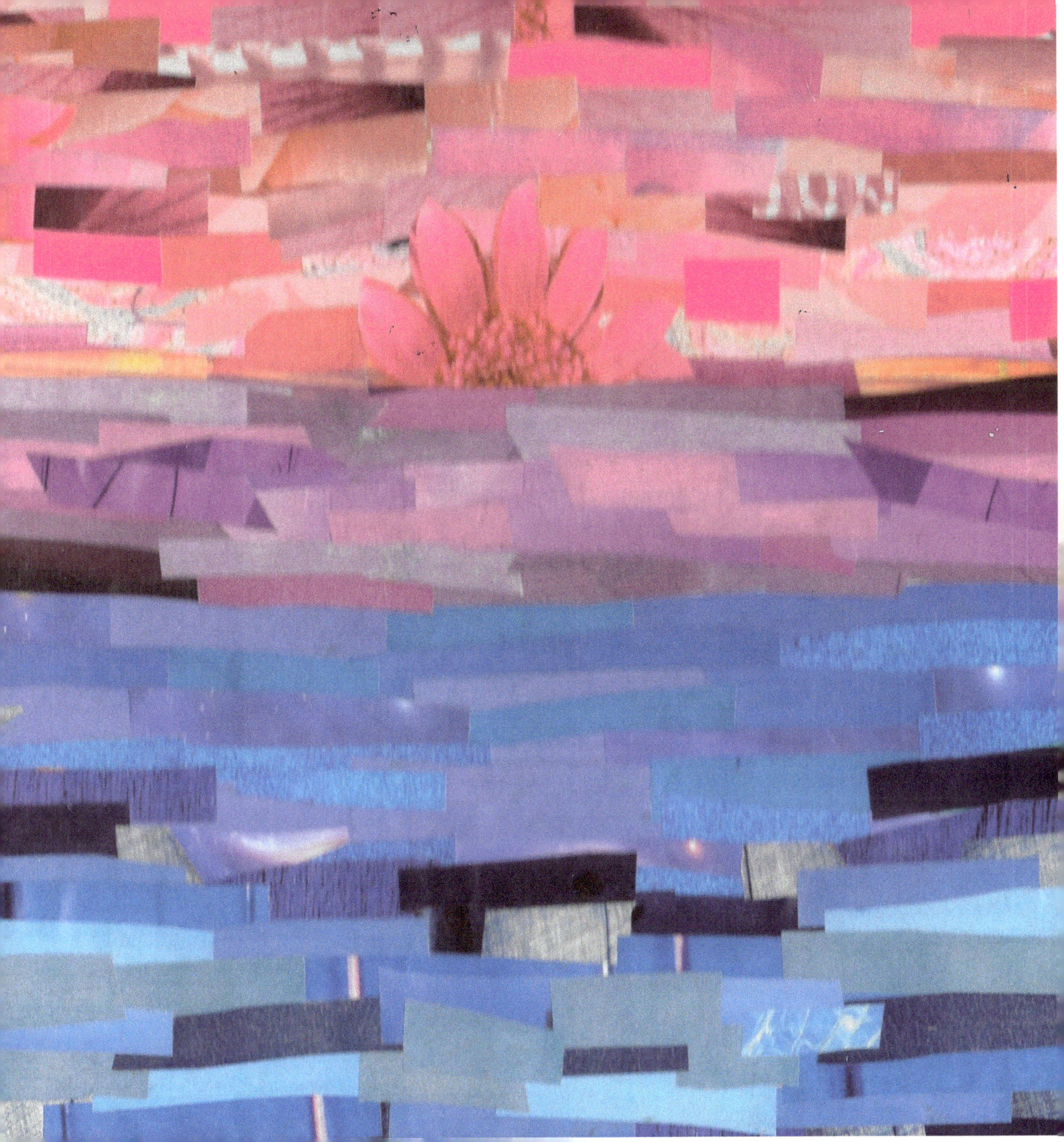

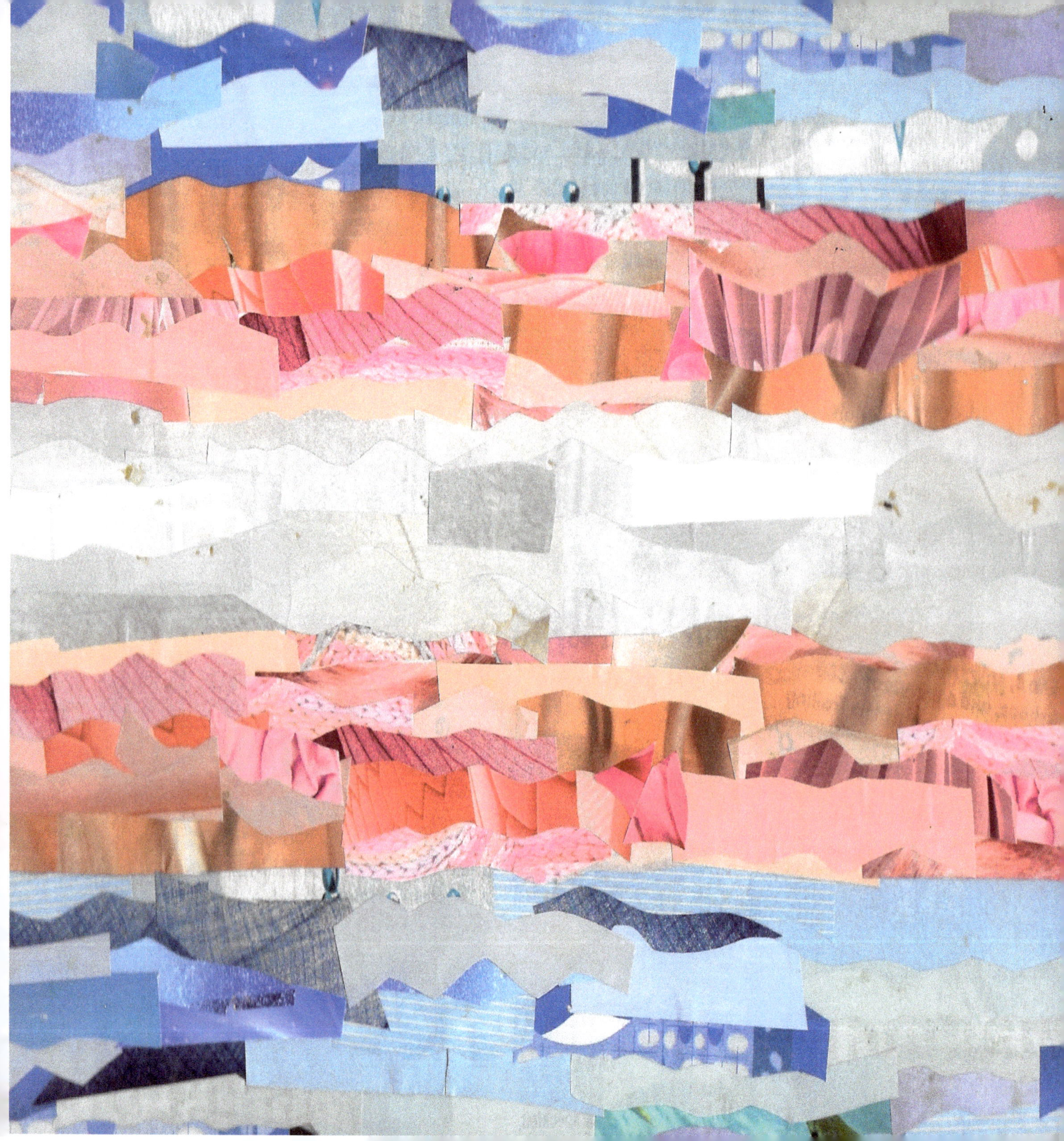

Transgender/Trans

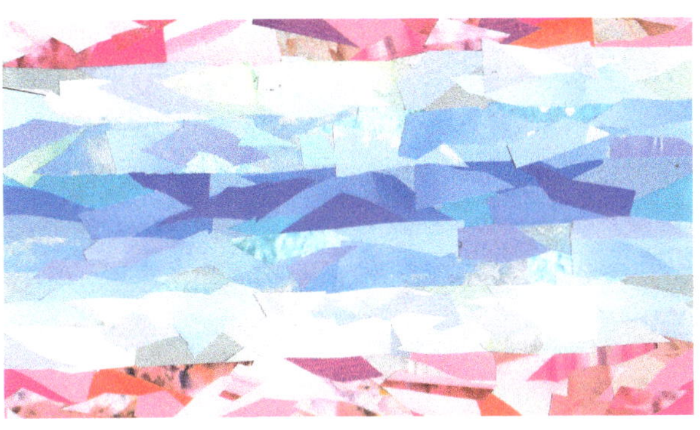

Transgender people are people who do not identify with their gender assigned at birth. This means they could identify as male, female, nonbinary, or any other gender they were not assigned at birth. Thus, there's a huge umbrella underneath the term transgender of not only trans men and trans women but also of anyone within the nonbinary community.

Being transgender looks different on people. Some people transition towards their gender if they wish to look more masculine, feminine, or androgynous. Others are happy to look as they already do. Some choose different pronouns than the ones others assume, some do not. Essentially: there is no wrong way for a person to be trans.

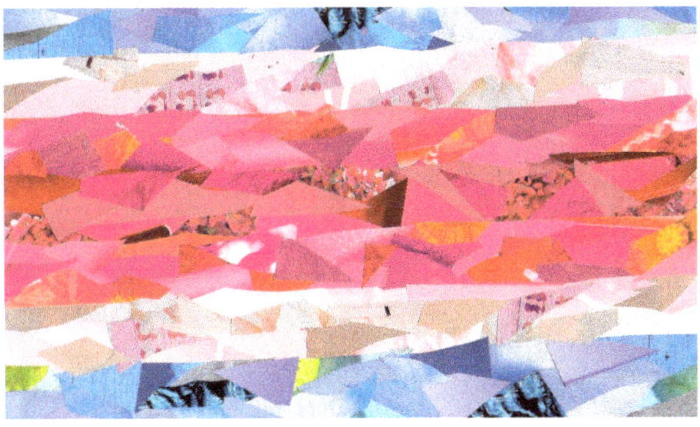

The blue stripes represent men, pink represent women, and white represents nonbinary people. The other two pride flags shown here are specifically for trans-masculine and transfeminine people, both with seven stripes. The transmasculine flag has one pink stripe and then light blue, blue, and a darker blue in the middle. The transfeminine flag has one blue stripe then light pink, pink, and a darker pink in the middle.

Well Known Transgender People: Laverne Cox (actress), James Barry (doctor who performed the first c-section), and Elliot Page (actor).

Queer

Queer is probably the least defined of any term within the Alphabet Soup of the LGBT+ community. It merely means that one identifies outside of heterosexual, heteroromantic, and cisgender. A convenient term for someone who has a complex identity, has not figured out exactly where they land, or merely wants a word that encapsulates them without further explanation.

Used as a slur for many years like many other parts of the community's terms (including lesbian and gay), it still hits an uncomfortable note for many, but others find comfort in it's ambiguity.

It is also generally considered more political than some other terms. "We're here, We're Queer, Get used to it" was a slogan popularized by Queer Nation and has been used to remind people that the LGBT+ community is not going anywhere.

Today, the flag is a queer chevron with one light purple and one dark purple arrow on a white background.

Well Known Queer People: Audre Lorde (Poet/Writer), Tessa Thompson (Actress), and Kehlani (Singer).

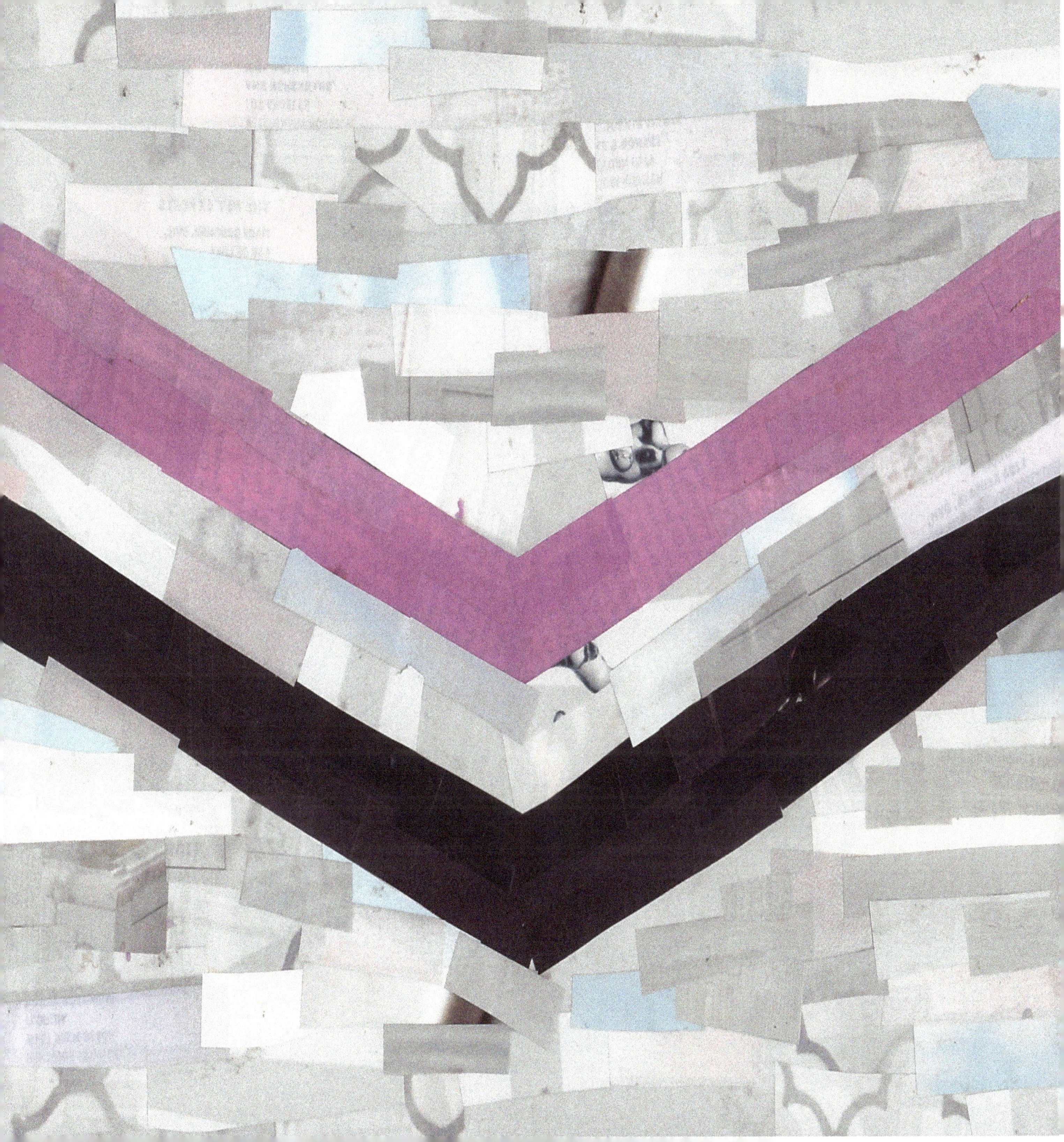

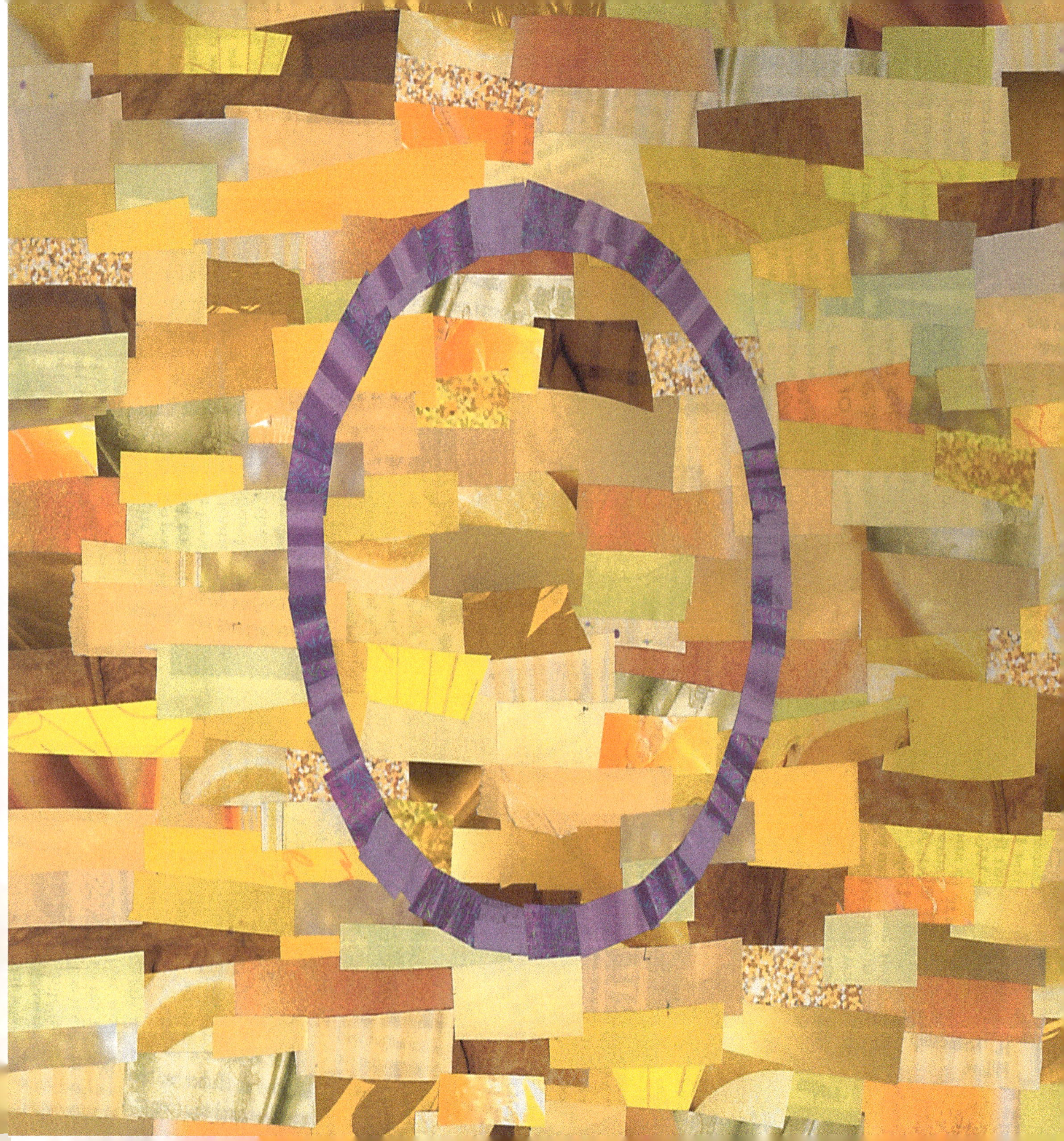

Intersex

Intersex people occupy a grey space in and outside of the LGBT+ community. Intersex is a genetic condition that means one's internal genes do not line up with their outward presentation or they have a difference between their internal and external sexual characteristics.[2] Since all children are currently assigned sex at birth, this can lead to some differences in gender identity and genetics than the person was assigned at birth.

Not all intersex people identify as part of the LGBT+ community, but some do and they continue to be a welcome part of the community.

The intersex flag is yellow with a purple circle and was created in 2013 using what is considered "hermaphrodite colors" and the purple central circle is "unbroken and unornamented, symbolising wholeness and completeness, and our potentialities." [3]

Well Known Intersex People: Caster Semenya (runner and Olympic gold medalist), Small Luk (Hong Kong activist), and Pidgeon Pagonis (writer and artist).

Asexual/Ace

Asexual people are people who do not experience sexual attraction. There is plenty of grey area between asexual and their allosexual counterparts that makes up what is commonly known as the ace spectrum.

Much like bi people, ace people are often excluded because of their identity not falling in one people traditionally recognize as LGBT+. Similarly, they can face discrimination and invalidation by both the LGBT+ community and straight people, especially those that do not understand how people can exist without sex.

Still, they continue to be a vibrant part of the community with their own long history. They also participate in relationship and sex sometimes, depending on the person. The important thing to remember is action does not equal attraction.

Aromantic asexual people are people who identify with both and often will use both terms unlike other identities who have matching romantic and sexual orientations.

The asexual pride flag is made up of black, grey, white, and purple stripes.

Well Known Aces: Yasmin Benoit (model and activist), Angela Chen (author), and Tim Gunn (fashion consultant).

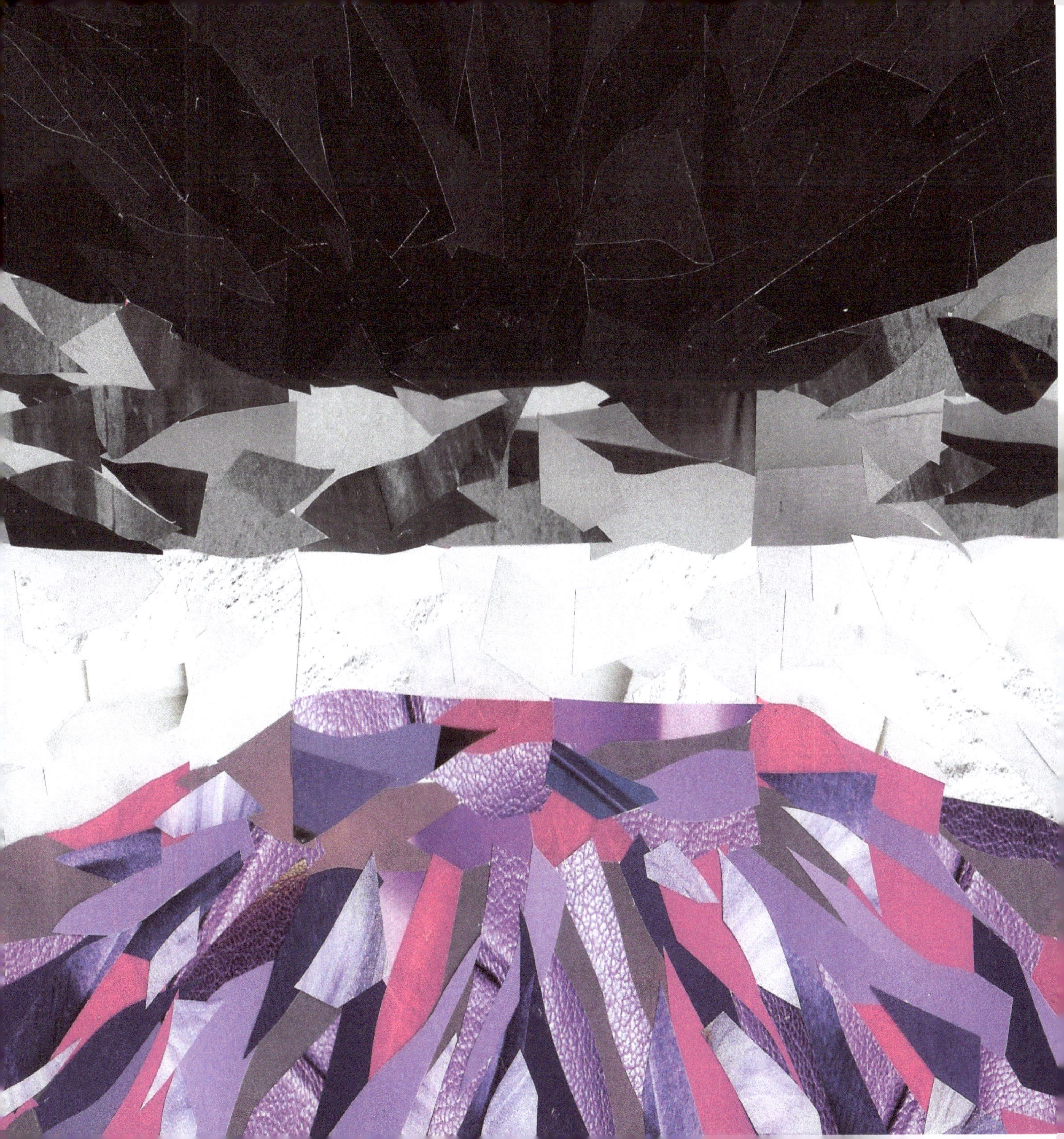

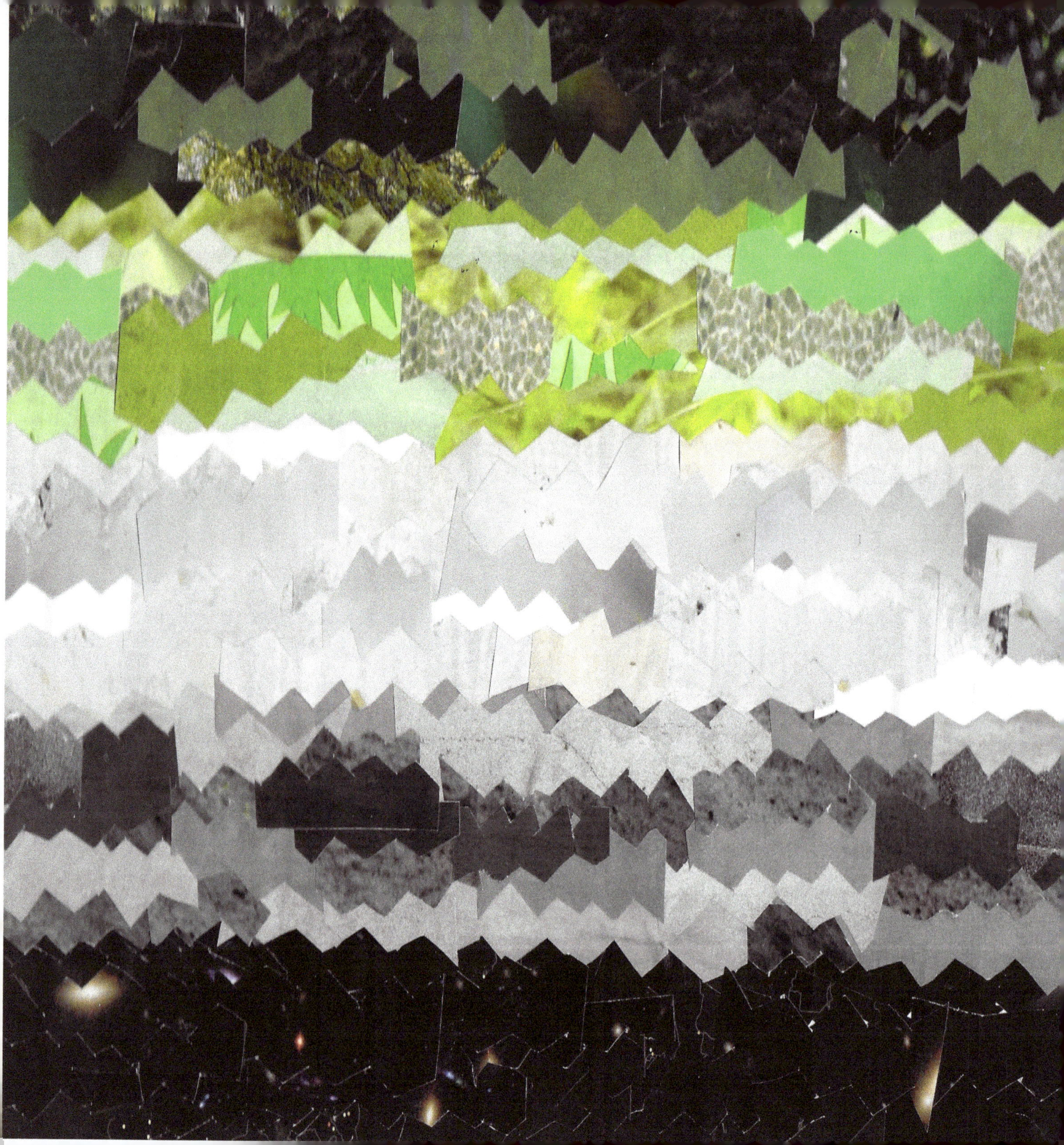

Aromantic/Aro

Aromantic people are people who do not experience romantic attraction. Like in asexuality, there is plenty of grey area between aromantic people alloromantic counterparts which makes up the aro spectrum.

Much like bi people, aro people are often excluded because of their identity not falling in one people traditionally recognize as LGBT+. Similarly, they can face discrimination and invalidation by both the LGBT+ community and straight people, especially those that do not understand how people can exist without romance.

An important note here is that some aromantics feel other kinds of love, like platonic love, and others prefer to leave the discussion of their general emotions out of it.

Still, they continue to be a vibrant part of the community with their own long history. They also participate in relationship and sex sometimes, depending on the person. Again, action does not equal attraction.

Aromantic asexual people are people who identify with both and often will use both terms unlike other identities who have matching romantic and sexual orientations.

The aro flag is five stripes of dark green, light green, white, grey, and black.

Well Known Aros: Alice Oseman (author) and Cavetown (songwriter).

Pan

Pansexual/panromantic is generally described as someone who is attracted to people regardless of gender. A common saying among pan people is "hearts not parts" as an example of their attraction.

Often, pan people and bi people can be lumped together with a number of other multi gender attraction labels. The differences between these identities are minute and often come down to person interpretation and preference.

The pan flag is three stripes of pink, yellow, and blue respectively.

Well Known Pans: JoJo Siwa (singer, dancer, actress), Brendan Urie (singer, songwriter), Jazz Jennings (activist).

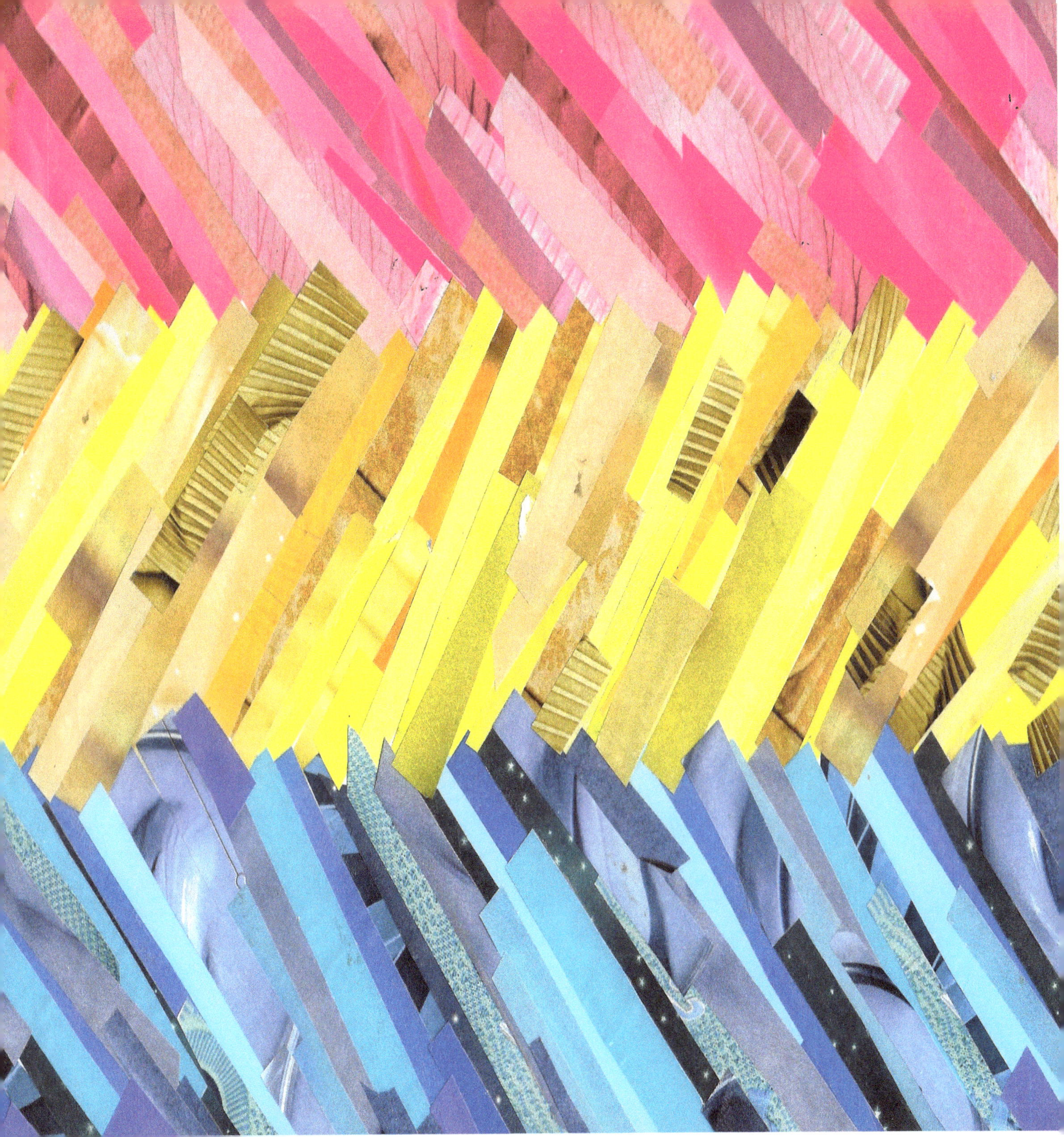

Nonbinary

Nonbinary people identify outside of just male or female. These people could be some level of androgynous, have a fluid gender, or identify with a third gender altogether.

People who are nonbinary often use different pronouns than the ones assigned at birth, or they may use multiple pronouns. He, she, they, or any number of neopronouns that are being used more and more commonly as ways many want to be referred to as.

A subsection of the transgender community, the nonbinary community also have many identities folded within it. Their gender presentation can vary and has no set look, meaning you won't always know if you're interacting with a nonbinary person just like you won't always know if you're interacting with a transgender person.

The nonbinary flag is equal stripes of yellow, white, purple, and black.

Well Known Nonbinary People: Demi Lovato (singer, actress), Rebecca Sugar (animator), Mauree Nivek Rajah Salima Turner (politician).

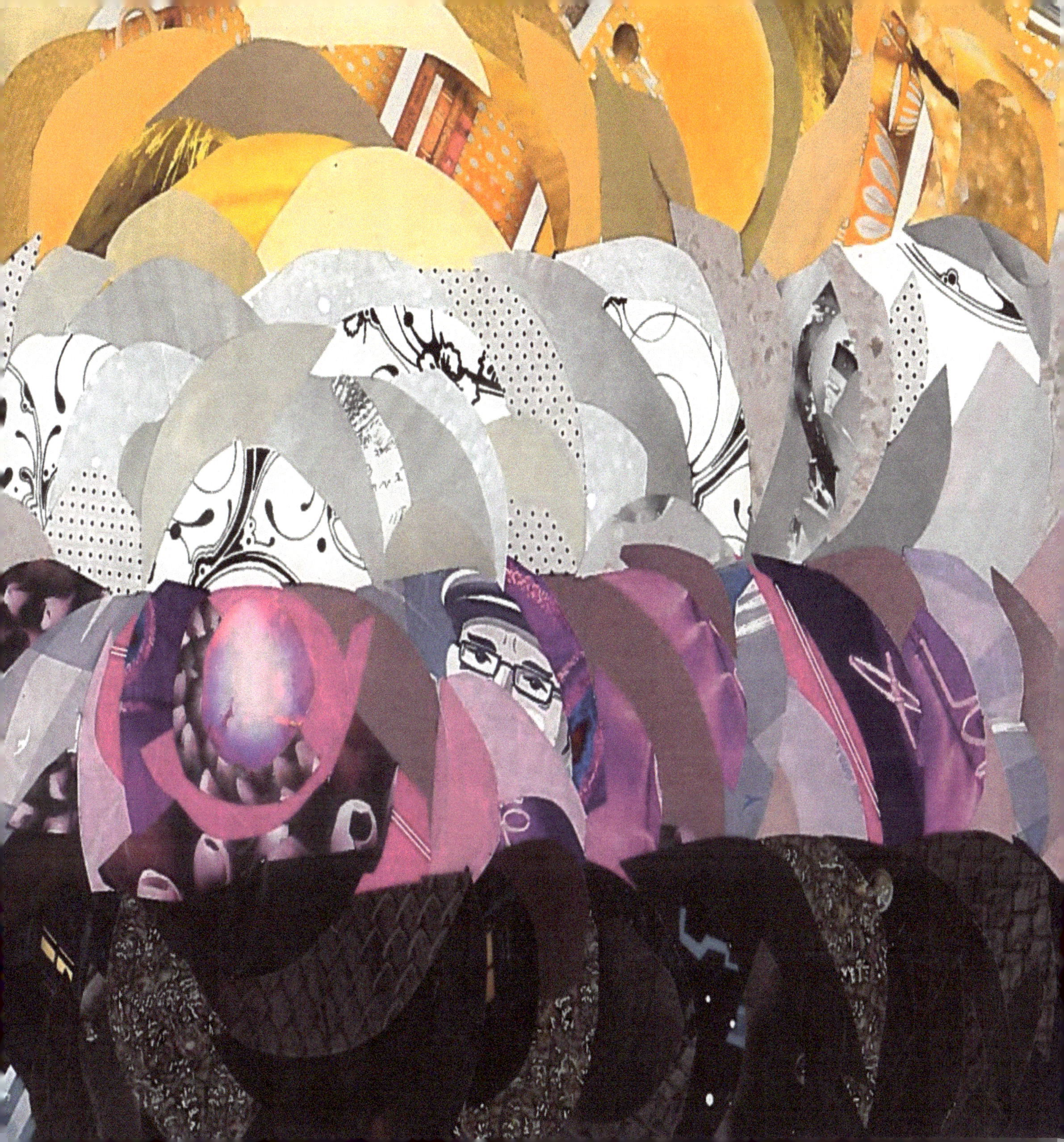

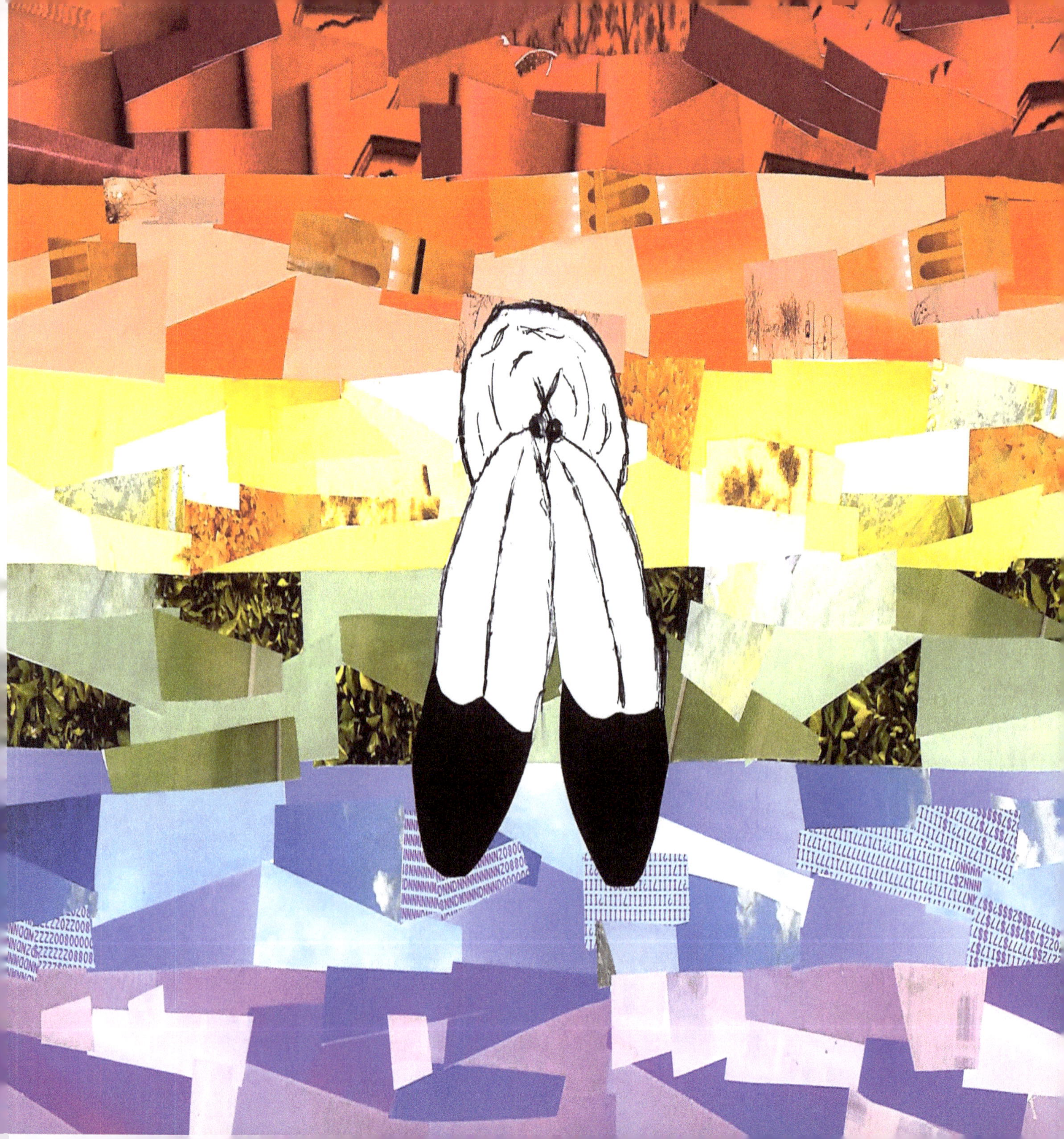

Two Spirit

A strictly Native American identity, two-spirit people are a third gender within some Native American communities.[4] They are typically recognized as someone of mixed gender in over 150 tribes in North America.

They were treated with great respect among their communities and took spouses of any gender depending on their preference. The two-spirit community continues to exist today across tribes the Americas much like gender diversity is recognized in many cultures across the world.

The Two Spirit flag is a six-stripe rainbow like the traditional LGBT+ pride flag with two feathers on the front.

Well Known Two-Spirit People: Susan Allen (politician), Smokii Sumac (poet), and Jeremy Dutcher (musician).

Chapter 3

Gender Identity Flags

The spectrum of gender goes far and wide. These flags cover some of the identities people use to describe themselves.

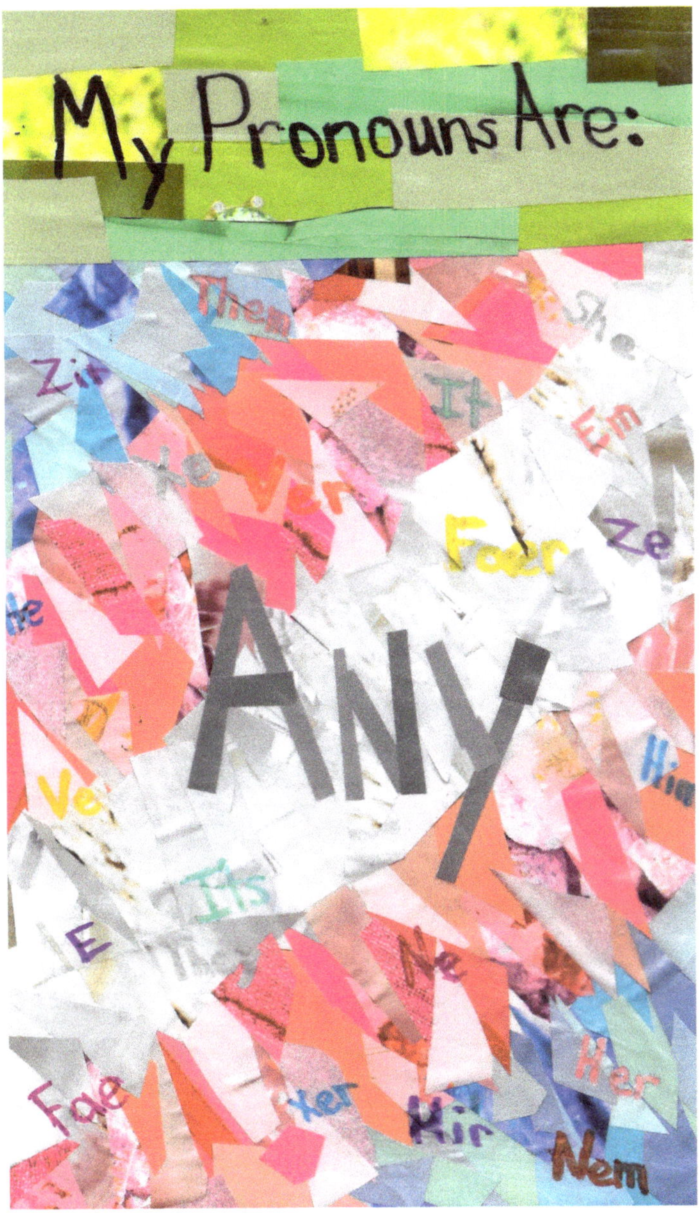
My Pronouns Are:
Them
She
Zir
It
Em
Xe
Ver
Faer
Ze
ANY
Ve
Its
E
Ne
Her
Fae
Xer
Hir
Nem

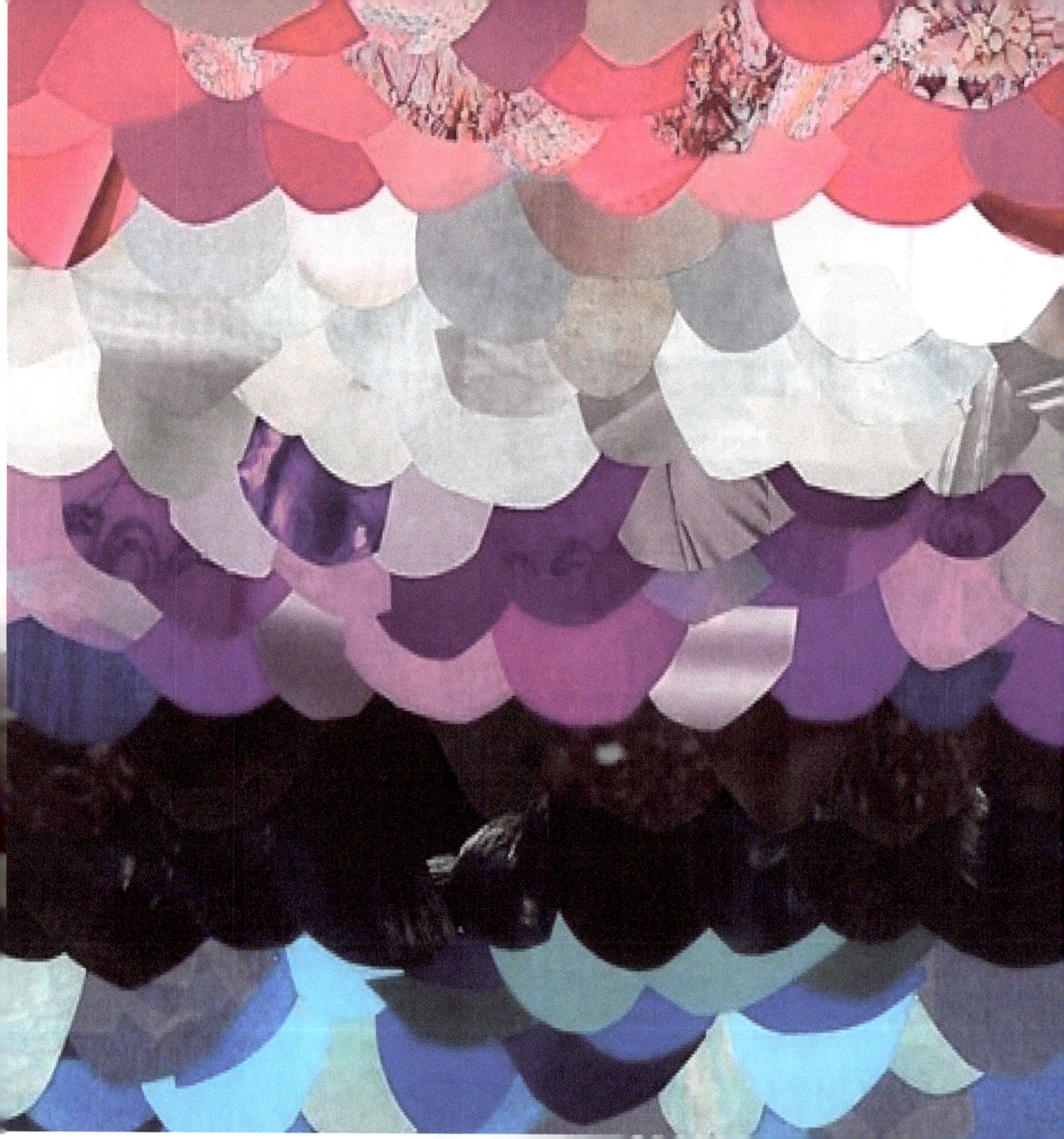

Genderfluid

Genderfluid people fall under the umbrella of transgender and nonbinary. These are people who's gender fluctuates between two or more points. This means that their identity is constantly shifting, making it much more fluid than most people's gender identities.

The spaces a person's identity is fluid between can vary. They can be fluid between male, female, androgynous, nonbinary, or any other point that they feel is relevant. How quickly it can shift also depends on the person with short spurts of different identities to much longer spurts. This means their pronouns might change regularly as well as their gender presentation.

Their pride flag is five stripes of pink, white, purple, black, and yellow.

Well Known Genderfluid People: Ruby Rose (actor), Alok Vaid-Menon (writer, performance artist).

Genderqueer

Genderqueer people do not subscribe to a traditional view of male or female whenever describing themselves, thus likely falling under the umbrella of nonbinary.

Much like the word queer, people who identify as genderqueer can fall among a variety of ways of identifying and presenting their gender. These people may be fluid in their gender or they may have something more consistently settled. It is a rather ambiguous term among the nonbinary and transgender community.

The genderqueer flag is three stripes of purple, white, and green.

Well Known Genderqueer People: Leo Baker (skate boarder), Johanna Hedva (artist and author), Maia Kobabe (cartoonist).

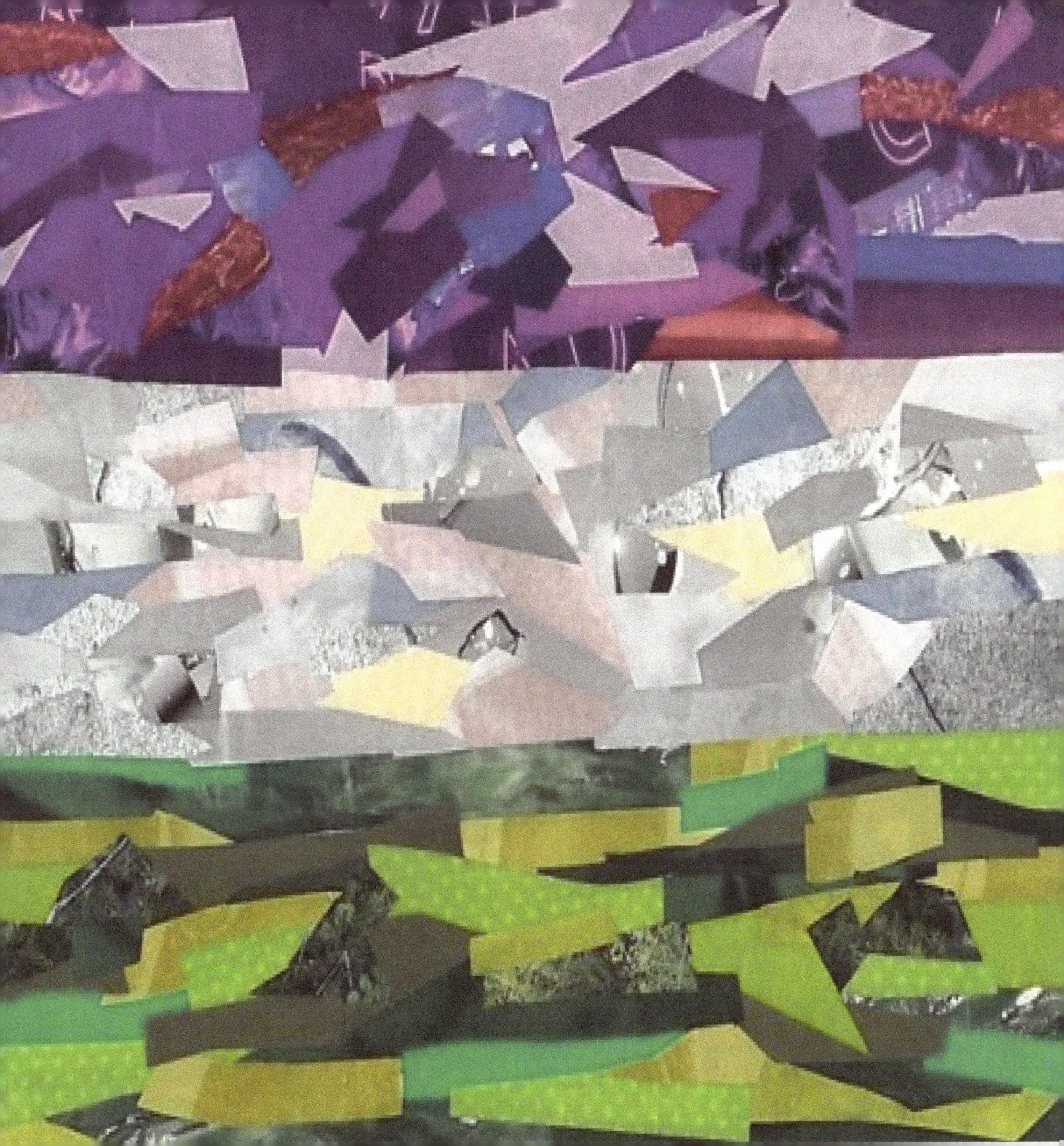

Bigender

Bigender is where a person experiences exactly two genders. Whether these genders are male and female or some combination of nonbinary and binary genders is another story that depends person to person.

Whether the person experiences their two genders at one time or flows back and forth also varies person to person.

The bigender flag is made up of seven stripes that range in a gradient from a dark pink to a dark blue with white in the middle.

Well Known Bigender Person: Rose Lemberg is a Ukrainian author and poet who is bigender.

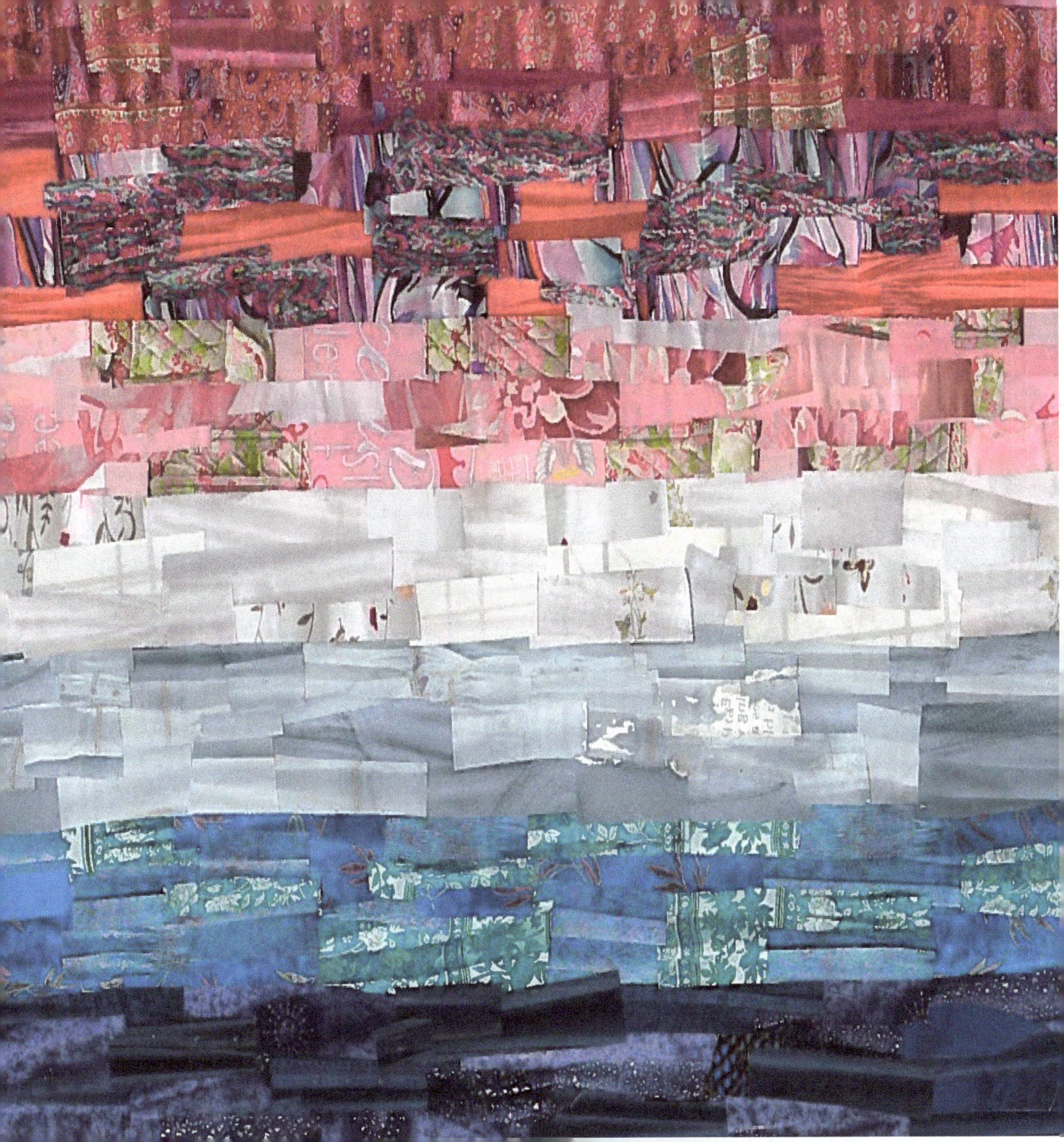

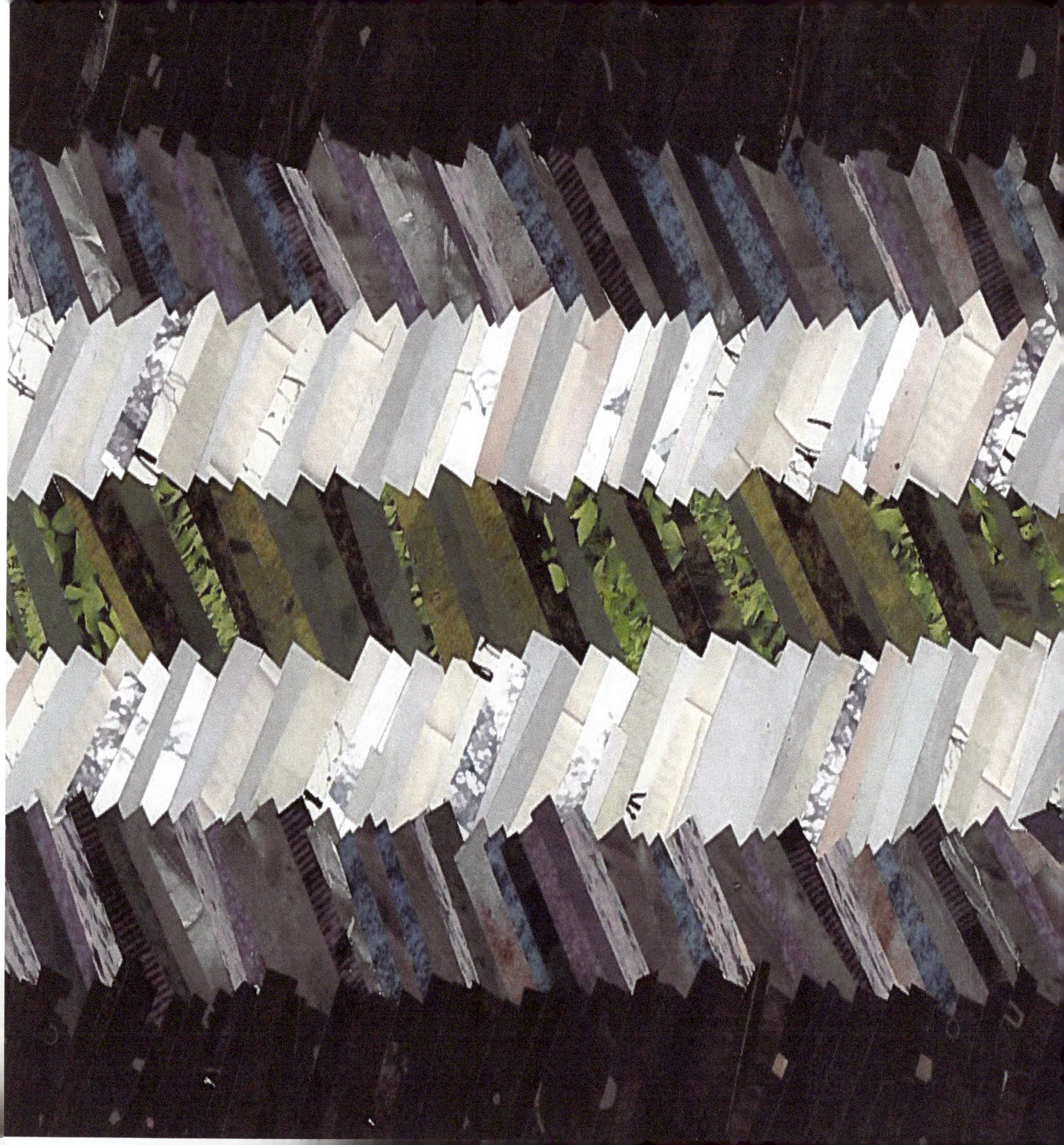

Agender

Agender is someone who does not identify with any gender on the binary spectrum between male and female. This is another nonbinary identity, though this one falls completely outside of male and female.

Much like when the a- prefix is used for romantic and sexual orientations, agender can mean someone who has no gender identity. While some may have managed to lose their identity in a game of cards, others identify as something beyond the binary. Either way, agender people fall under the transgender and nonbinary umbrellas.

The agender flag is seven stripes which are black, grey, white, green, white, grey, and black.

Well Known Agender Person: Angel Haze (rapper).

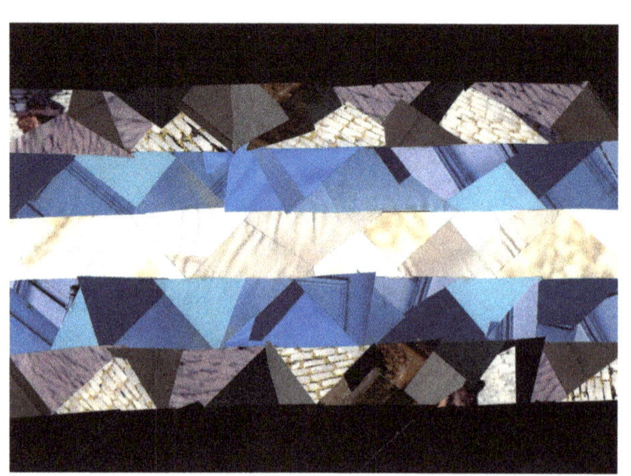

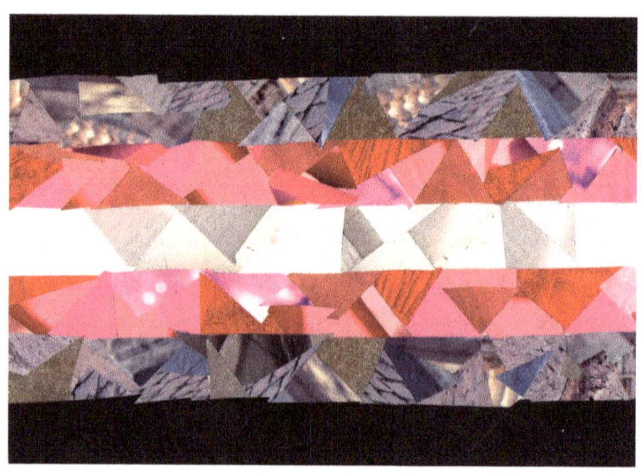

Demi-guy/Demi-girl/Demi-gender

Demi guys and girls are people who do not feel fully at home within the gender identity of man or woman, they are only partially there. Hence, demi. They may or may not identify as another gender as well, that depends person to person.

These can be nonbinary or transgender identities as the person does not necessarily identify partially with the gender they were born with. Both of these do fall under the spectrum of demigender which is someone who only partially experiences a gender.

Demi-gender is the umbrella term for people who may fall within this category as they would be someone who partially connects to a gender identity, like man or woman, but does not full connect.

The three flags are made up of seven stripes. From the outside to the middle, they go black; grey; then blue for demi-guy, pink for demi-girl, and yellow for demi-gender; and white in the middle.

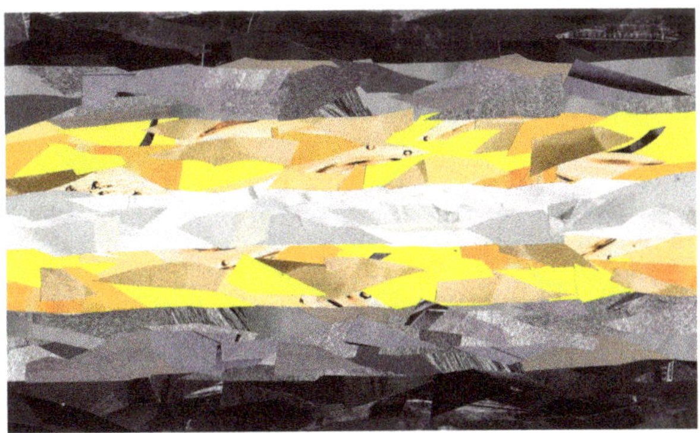

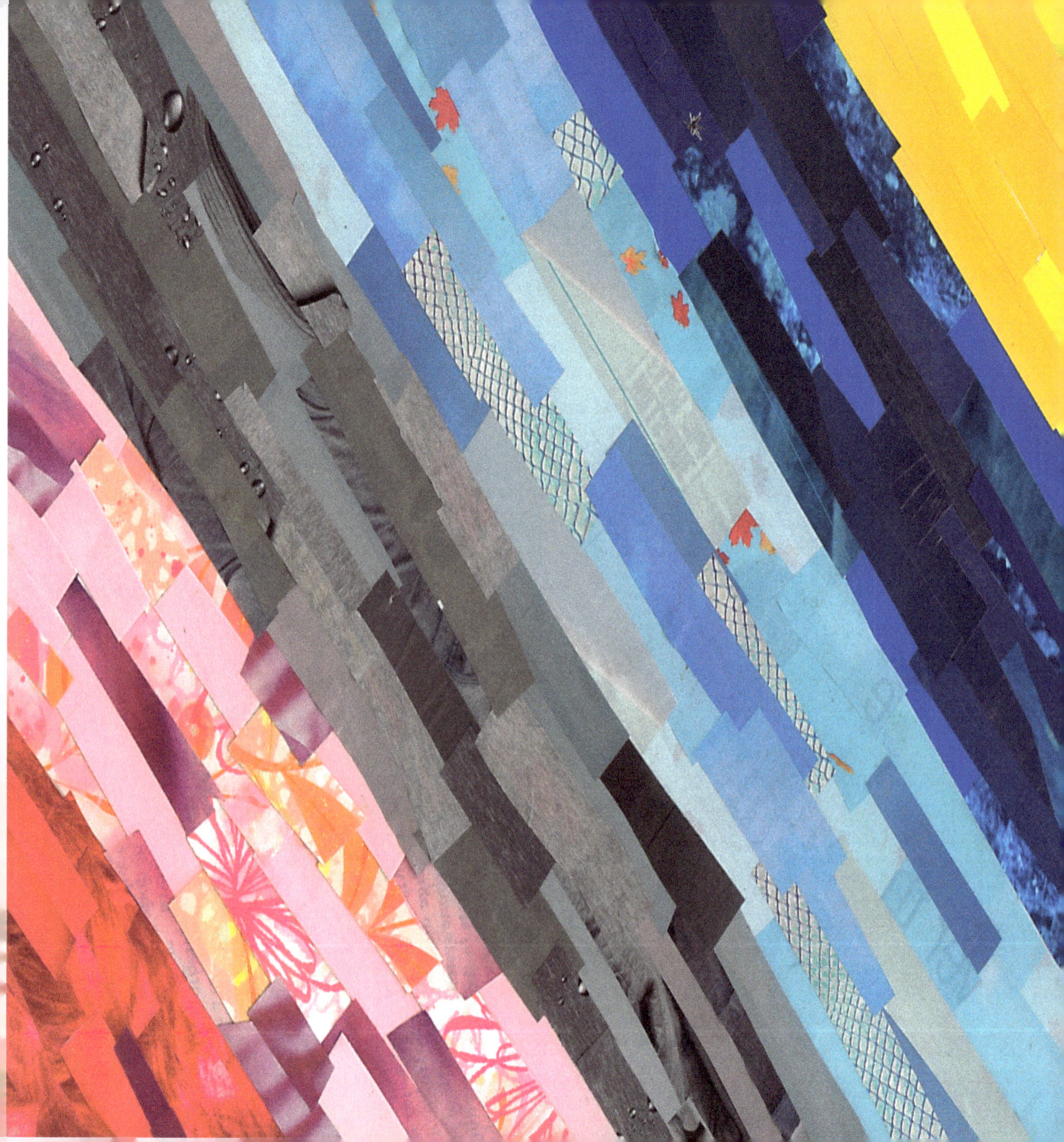

Genderflux

Genderflux is a term people use when their gender fluctuates in intensity. It somewhat like genderfluid but usually with one gender that ranges from that gender identity at 100% all the way down to 0% gender identity where the person may be nearly agender.

Generally, a genderflux person will only have one gender they fluctuate into rather than multiple, thought not always.

While not as well known as many of it's nonbinary and transgender counterparts, it has been around for a while and gained more visibility with a Teen Vogue article in 2016.[5]

There are several versions of the genderflux flag. The one pictured here is six stripes of dark pink, pink, grey, light blue, blue, and yellow.

Abrogender

Abrogender is when someone experiences gender so quickly that it cannot be pinned down or having such a broad gender experience that they feel like they are constantly discovering what their gender means to them. This falls under the non-binary and transgender umbrella for many people as the person's gender can fluctuate very quickly.

On some occasions, it is seen as a subsection of genderfluid when the person experiences multiple genders very quickly.

The abrogender flag is made up of five stripes which are blue, green, white, purple, and black.

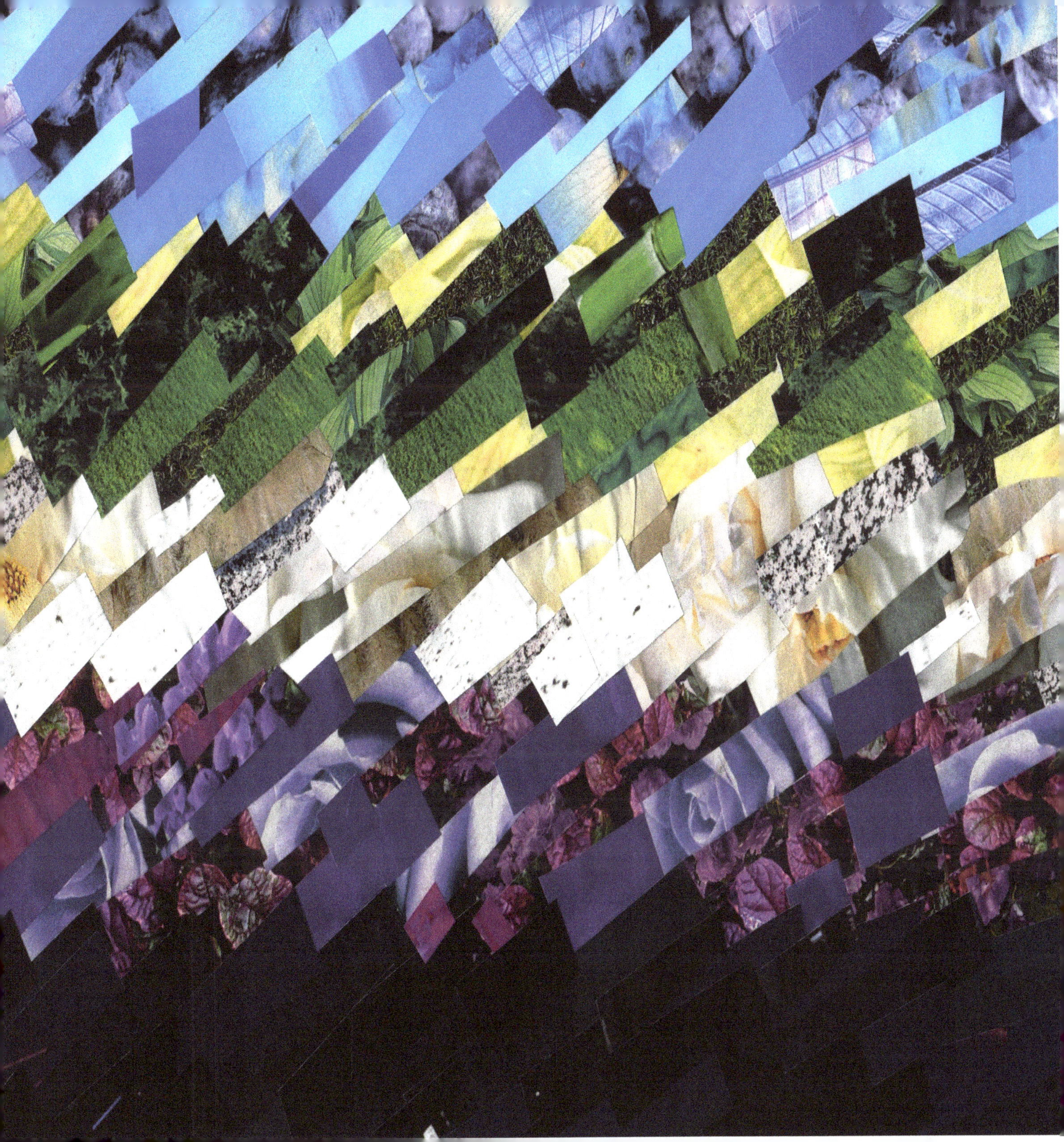

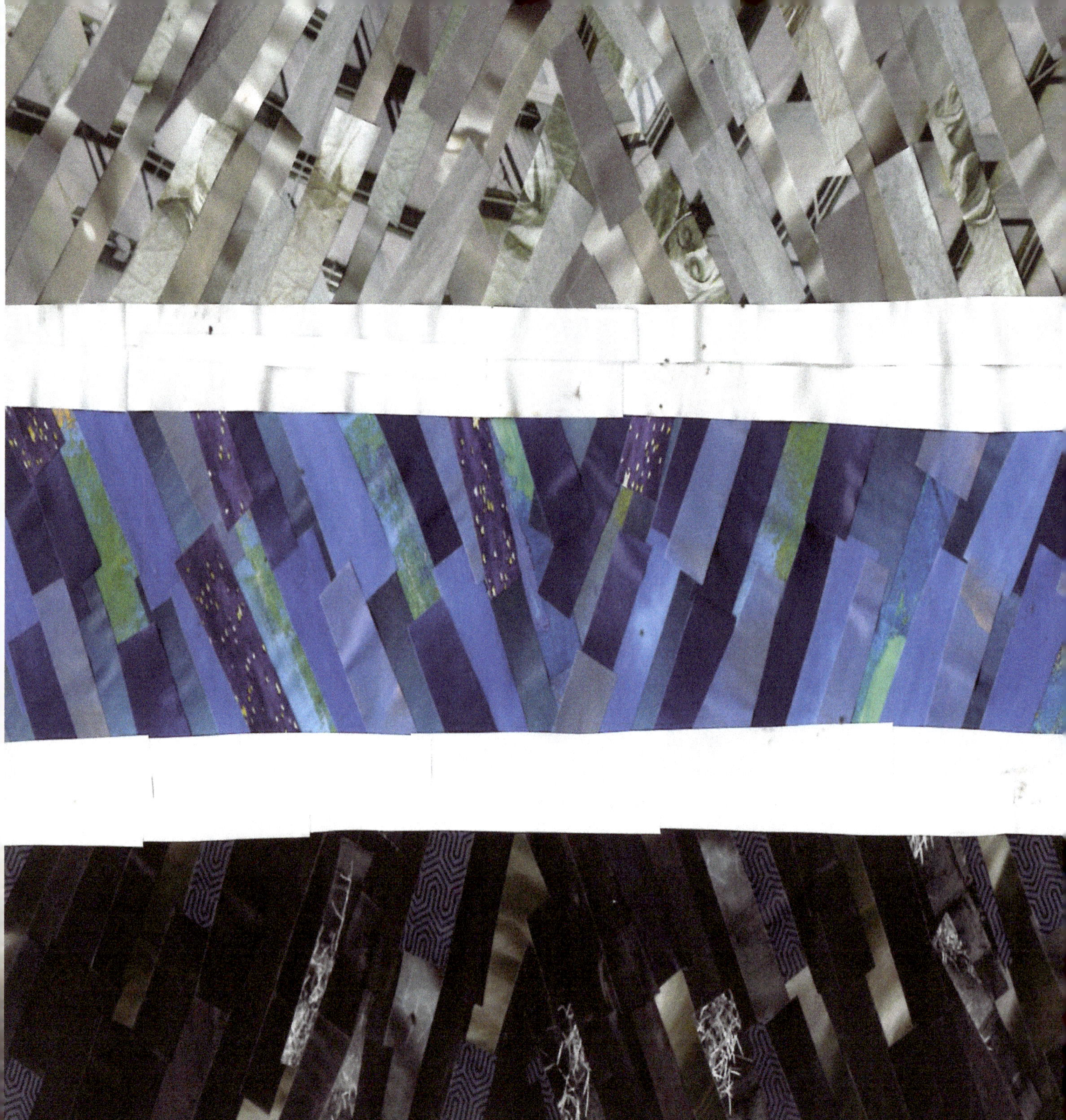

Greygender

Greygender is a bit like the other side of demi-guy and demi-girl. Someone who is greygender identifies partially with being nonbinary and partially with something else, whether they name that something else or not. They may not have a strong attachment to any gender label but feel like they do experience gender, unlike some agender people.

Their gender experience may be weak or almost unnoticeable sometimes, and it can be anywhere on the spectrum of nonbinary genders.

The greygender flag is five stripes. There are three equal sized stripes of grey, blue, and black with thin white stripes between them.

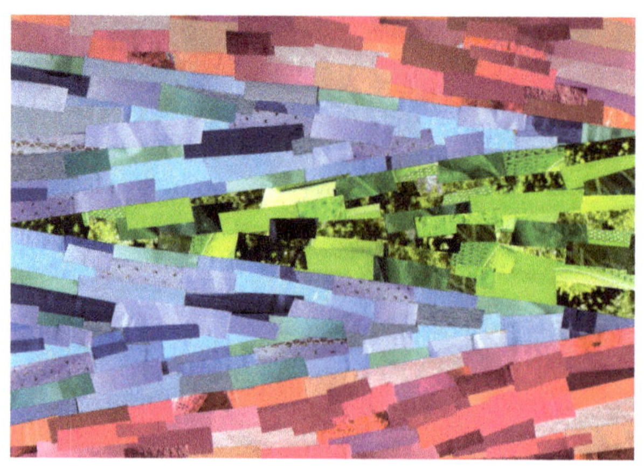

Trigender

Trigender is much like bigender in that someone experiences more than one gender, though this one specifically refers to experience three genders. This could be all three at once or a more fluid identity between three specific genders.

This is a nonbinary and transgender identity as there are only two genders within the binary, so the person needs at least one gender in the middle or outside of the binary.

The trigender flag is five stripes of pink, blue, green, blue, and pink.

Pangender

Pangender is a broader form of bigender and trigender where the person experiences multiple genders but not necessarily a set number. Like those identities, this could be a fluid gender identity between someone's gender identities or something more simultaneous.

This identity falls under the category of nonbinary and transgender. Essentially, a pangender person experiences two or more genders.

Pangender can have a lot in common with other multigender identities since it is such a broad term. Much like the differences between bisexual, pansexual, and multi attraction labels, this is similar in the sense of people will pick whatever they feel the most in touch with as the differences between them can be very small.

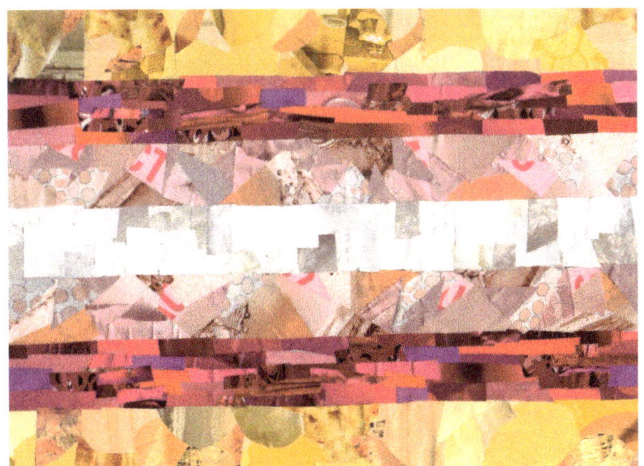

The pangender flag is made up of seven stripes that are yellow, dark pink, light pink, white, light pink, dark pink, and yellow.

Polygender

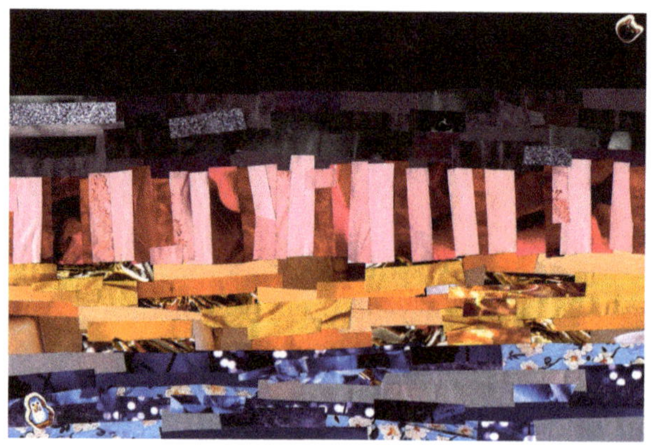

Polygender is when someone experiences multiple genders, much like trigender, bigender, and pangender. These can be all at once or a fluctuation between the genders. There is no limit on how many genders a person who is polygender may experience, much like pangender.

This is a nonbinary and transgender identity as the person does not identify solely or at all with the gender they were born with. It can look different on every person as every person will likely experience polygender differently.

The polygender flag is five stripes of black, grey, pink, yellow, and blue.

Quoigender

Using the French for the word "what", Quoigender people have a gender identity that is too complex to either label with existing terminology or someone who is done with examining their gender to the point of wanting to lack a label. It is also used by people who aren't sure they experience a gender at all.

This term can be used by people under other umbrella terms as they please. People also use it to signify that they are questioning their gender sometimes because their gender has become a question mark for themselves as they try to understand themselves further.

Either way, quoigender people tend to have a complex gender identity. This is the current term when the original one was more known as WTFgender, much like the counterpart for quoiromantic and quoisexual being WTFsexual.

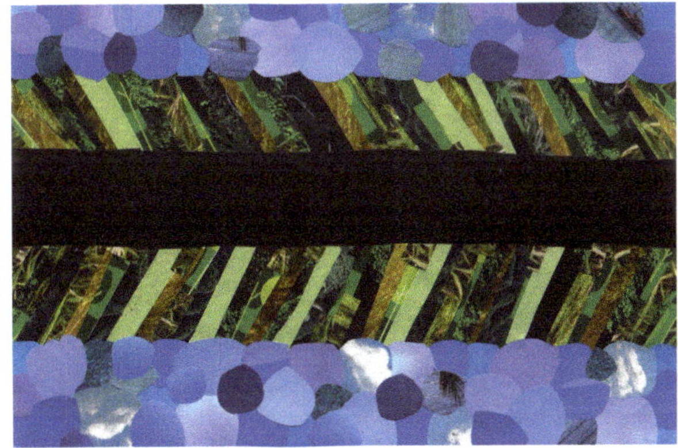

The quoigender flag is five stripes of blue, green, black, green, and blue.

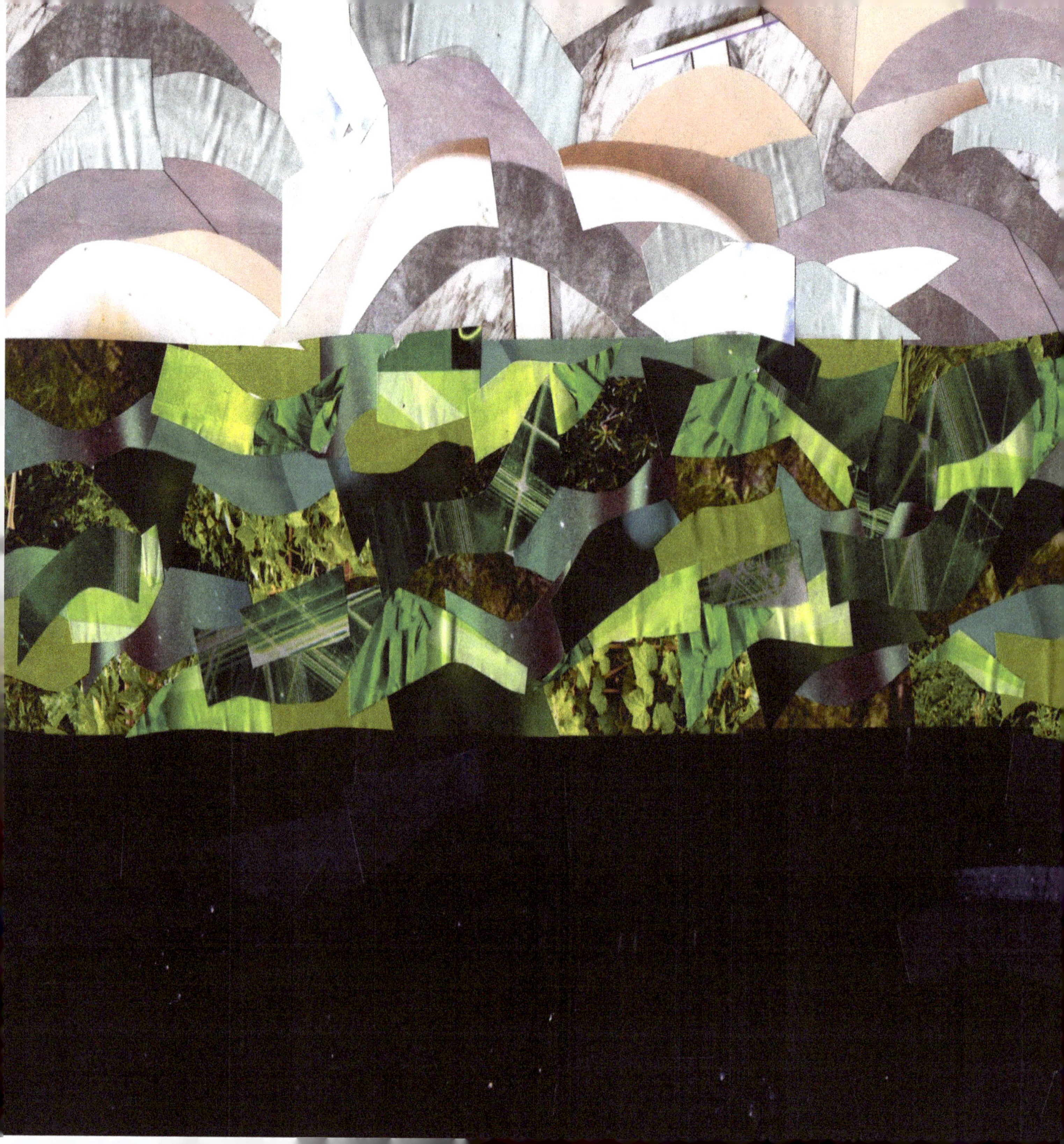

Neutrois

Neutrois people identify as something that is null or neutral, many they completely lack gender or their gender is quite neutral. Thus, this is an identity that falls under the nonbinary and transgender umbrellas.

People who identify this way tend to have quite a bit of overlap with agender people. This is because both can experience a complete lack of gender that leaves them far outside the gender binary or in the realm of a third gender like some other nonbinary people.

Often, experiencing gender dysphoria is a common experience of neutrois people. While this occurs in other trans and nonbinary identities, it is particularly noted among sources that neutrois people may try to change their gender presentation towards something far more neutral.[6]

Neutrois is made up of three equal stripes of white, green, and black.

Potential Historical Figure Who May Have Been Neutrois: Public Universal Friend was a Quaker preacher in the late 1700s and early 1800s who identified as completely genderless.[7]

Androgyne

Androgyne as a gender identity very closely associated with androgyny. It is a non-binary identity which is simultaneously male and female in varying degrees depending on the person.

Like other nonbinary identities, people who are androgyne may seek to change their gender presentation through dress and medical means. They also may seek to change their gender marker where possible to an X rather than an F or M.

The androgyne flag is three vertical trips of pink, purple, and blue.

Well Known Androgyne People: Jennie June was the first transgender person to write and publish an autobiography in the US called *The Autobiography of an Androgyne*. Alex MacFarlane was the first person to use an X gender marker on a passport.

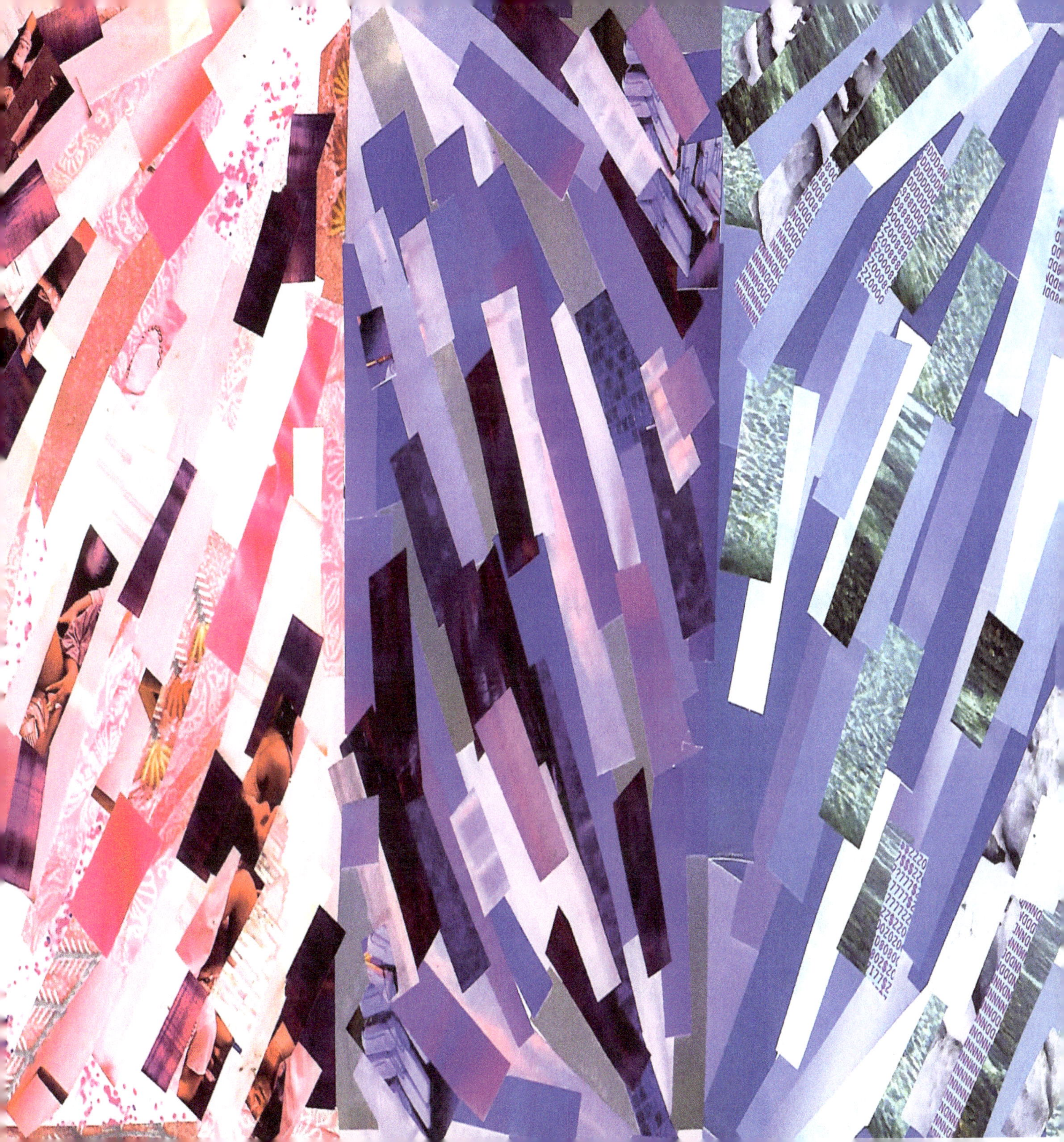

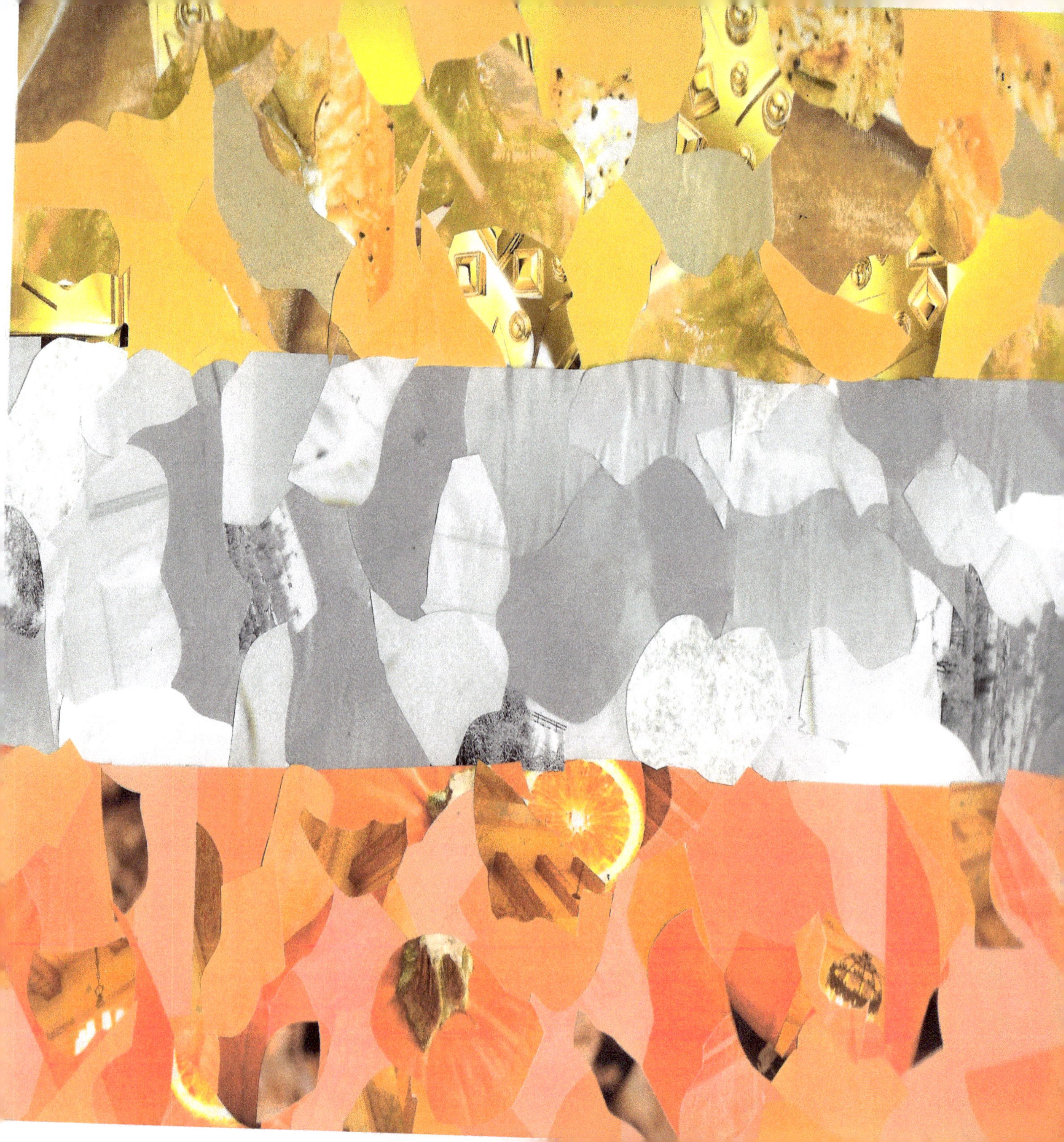

Maverique

Maverique people experience gender and do not have apathy towards it, but their gender is completely independent from female, male, or nonbinary. Maverique people can be multigender, but that not necessary. Their gender is derived from something else completely.

This complete lack of association with other genders means that it can be harder to pin down than many nonbinary or transgender identities. There can be some overlap with other gender identities which means sometimes people will identify as maverique and another gender or as solely maverique.

The maverique flag is made up of a yellow, white, and orange stripe.

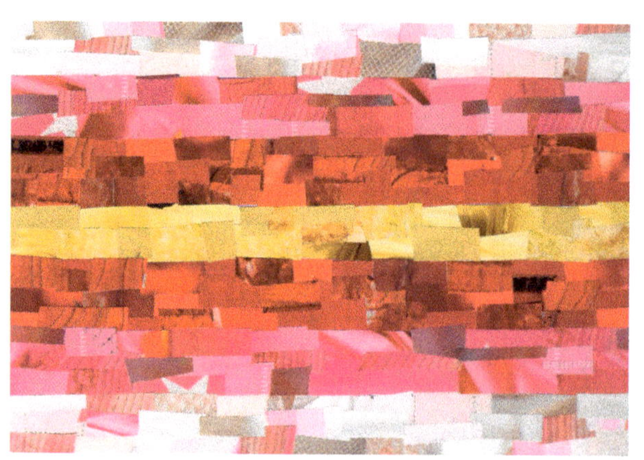

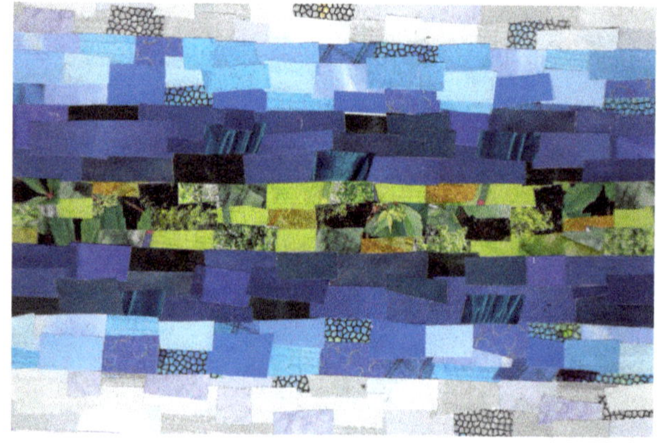

Girlflux/Boyflux

Girflux and Boyflux is for people who fluctuate between being a boy or a girl and having almost no gender. This is mostly about the intensity of the person's gender ranging from 0% to 100% of one gender.

A person who identifies with either of these may be a nonbinary or transgender identity for the person, especially considering that the person will range into a nonbinary or agender area with their fluctuating gender.

The girflux flag is seven stripes of light pink, pink, dark pink, yellow, dark pink, pink, and light pink. The boyflux pride flag is seven stripes of light blue, blue, dark blue, green, dark blue, blue, and light blue. These both represent the fluctuating identity the person using these labels experiences.

Chapter 4

Lesser Known LGBT+ Identity and Microlabels

Haven't heard of these identities? You aren't alone. This section is going to cover identities that tend not to be as well known but are just as important as the ones everyone knows.

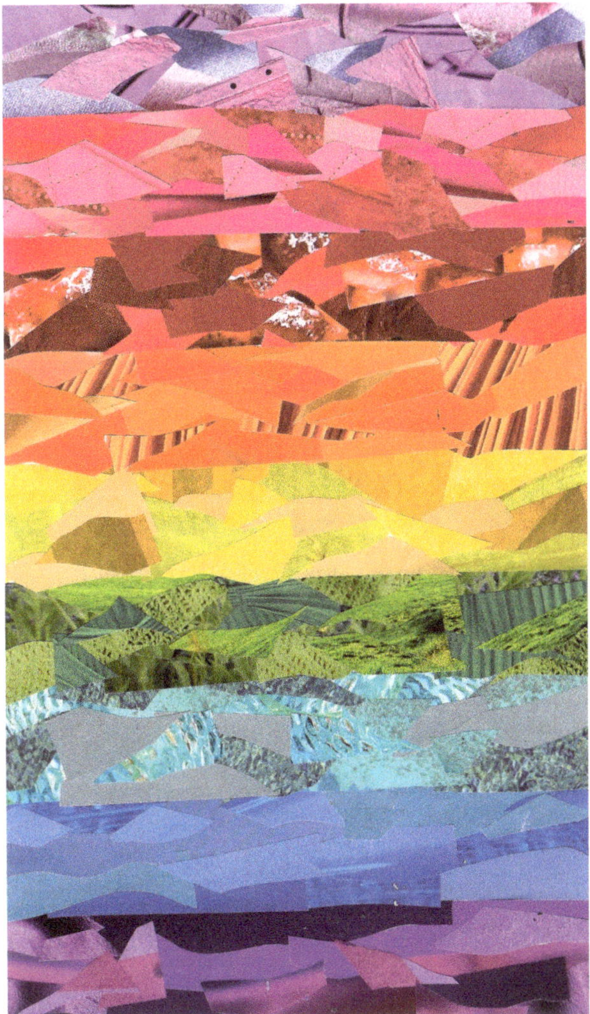

This is a variation of Gilbert Baker's 8 stripe pride flag which is very similar to his original. This 9 stripe version has a lavender stripe on top to celebrate the diversity of the LGBT+ community.

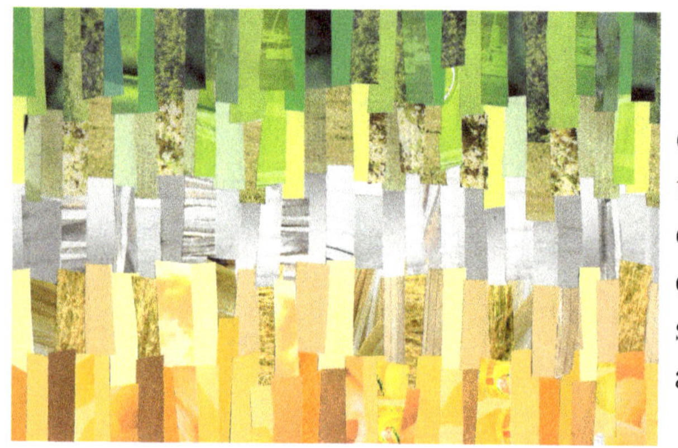

Alloace and Alloaro

Alloace and Alloaro are people that do not identify as aromantic and asexual. They experience split attraction with either a different sexual and romantic orientation. This means they will experience some form of attraction that aromantic and asexual people will not.

Usually, people within these communities will use another descriptor to describe the other part of their identity like homoromantic, pansexual, heterosexual, or any other number of terms that fall within the spectrum of attraction.

Heteroromantic asexuals and aromantic heterosexuals are still just as welcome within the LGBT+ community because they do not fall within what society has dictated to be the average person. Not all of these people will consider themselves as part of the LGBT+ community, but they have a space here just like everyone else

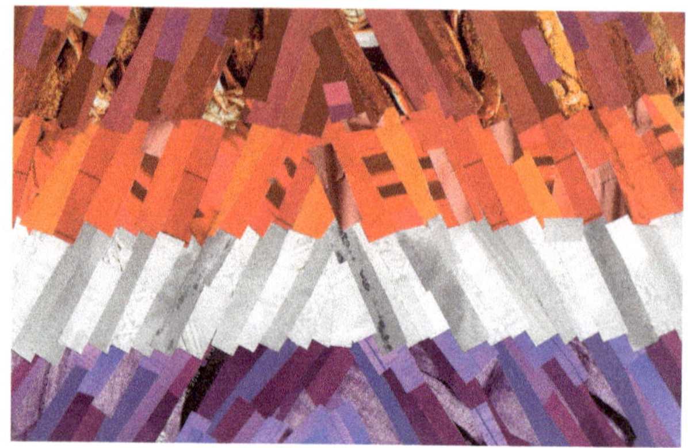

The stripes of dark red, red, white, and purple flag is for alloace people. The green to yellow gradient flag with five stripes is for alloaro people.

Aceflux/Aroflux

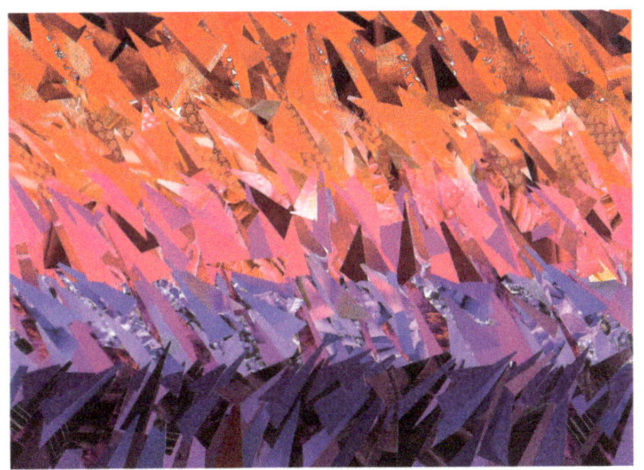

Aceflux (asexual flux) and Aroflux (aromantic flux) people fluctuate between another orientation to aromantic or asexual. This can be paired with any other orientation by the person who identifies this way or be used on its own, much like other aro and ace spectrum orientations.

Orientation can fluctuate for a lot of people no matter what their identity. However, aceflux and aroflux tend to consistently fluctuate from other orientations or attractions to aromantic and

asexual. This is usually more consistent than people who switch to use another label.

Someone who is aceflux may not identify as aroflux and vice versa.

Both flags have five stripes. The aceflux flag is a gradient from red to purple. The aroflux flag is a gradient from red to green.

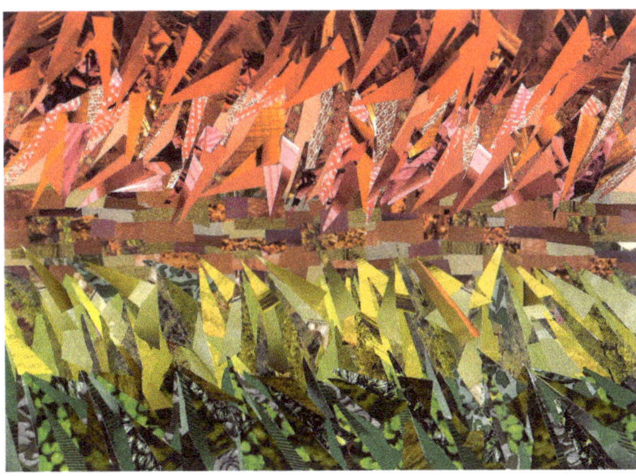

Achillean

Achillean people are men or male aligned people who are attracted to other men or male aligned people. They may be attracted to other genders and alignments as well, but they are also men loving men (or MLM, not to be confused with Multi Level Marketing schemes, which can be quite confusing). Other terms can be apollian, chaeronean, or wildean.

This term came from the Greek myth of Achilles. While the myth is about his feats as a warrior, Achilles was a man who may have been attracted to other men. In his case, it is speculated Achilles and Patroclus were lovers.

It can be combined with any other number of labels for someone's identity as someone may be attracted to more than just men or male aligned people. A man may also identify as gay as well as achillean.

The achillean pride flag is two light blue stripes with a white stripe in the middle. The white stripe contains a green carnation. There are other versions of the achillean pride flag, but this is generally recognized as the most commonly used one.

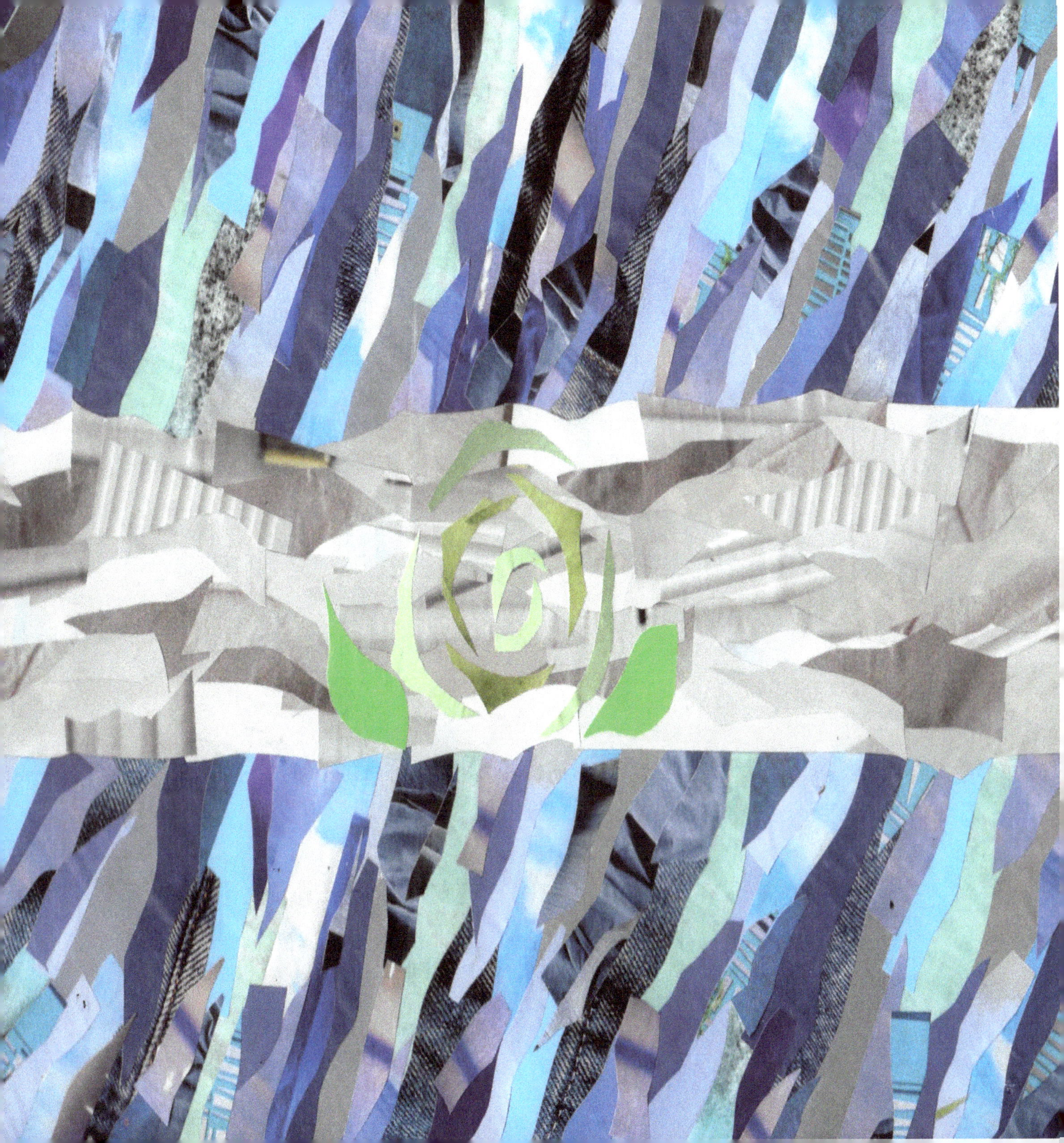

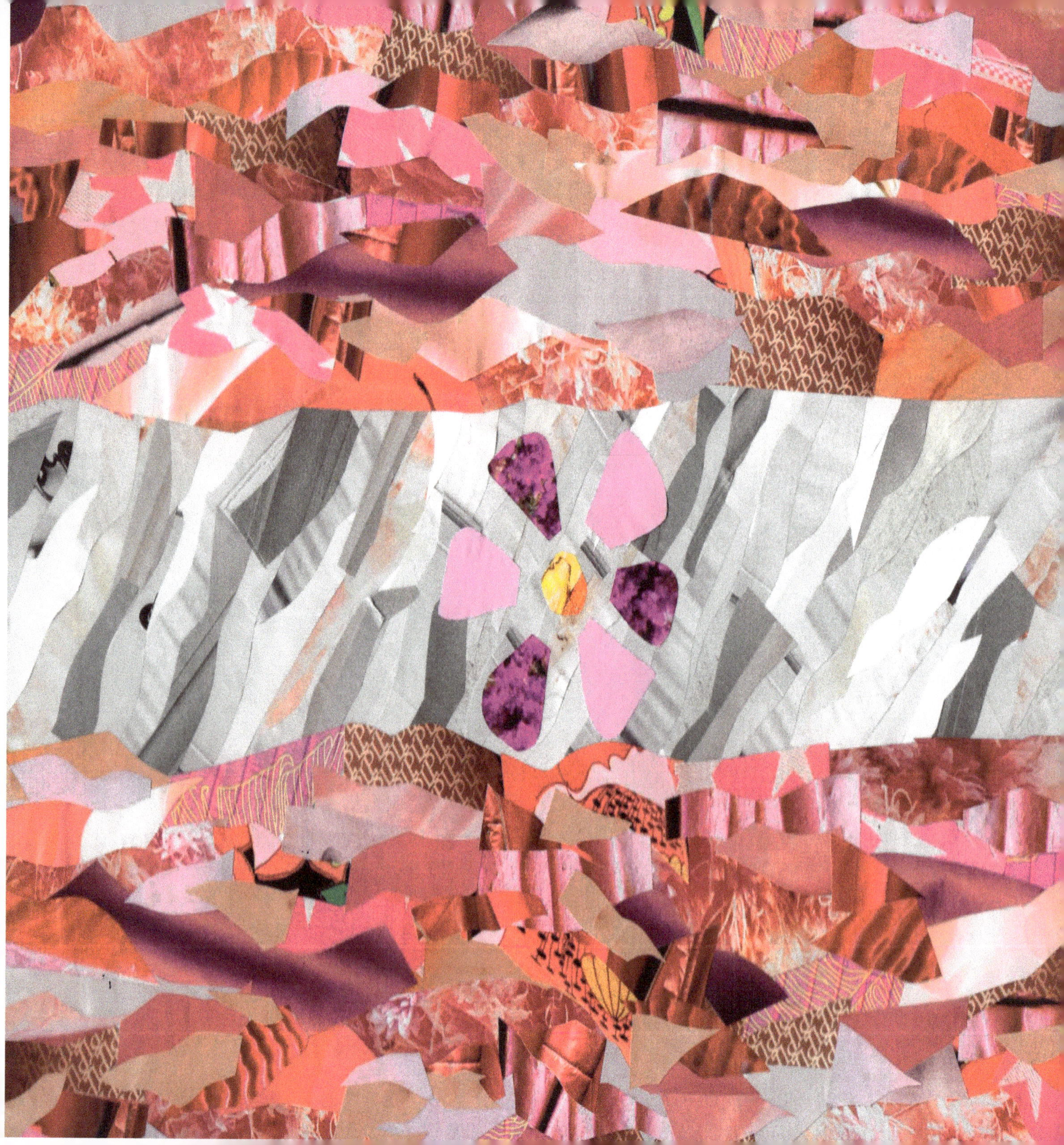

Sapphic

Sapphic is when a woman or woman aligned person is attracted to other women or women aligned people. Like achillean, people who use this term may experience attraction to other genders as well.

The word sapphic is based off the Greek poet Sappho who lived in the 600s and 500s BC. What survives of her poetry discusses her love for women. She was born on the isle of Lesbos, which is where the word lesbian comes from.

Her poem 'Awed by Her Splendor' reads:

Awed by her splendor
stars near the lovely
moon cover their own
bright faces
when she
is roundest and lights
earth with her silver

The sapphic flag is two pink stripes with a white stripe in the middle. The white stripe contains a violet which is a symbol of women loving women.

Diamoric

Diamoric is a term like sapphic or achillean. The word refers to nonbinary people who do not identify under a same/other gender attraction dichotomy due to being non-binary and not fitting under gay or straight. They may also be attracted to a number of genders, so people who are diamoric could also be attracted to men, women, or other nonbinary people. Other terms for people who might identify with diamoric include adonian, adonic, cypric, or dionysian.

This word was created using Greek as it's source language, much like sapphic and achillean, where the prefix dia- means "love that crosses through, goes apart from, or entirely encompasses the gender spectrum."[8]

The pride flag most commonly seen is three strips. The top and bottom stripes are a light green and the middle strip is white. In the middle stripe, there is a purple myrtle flower.

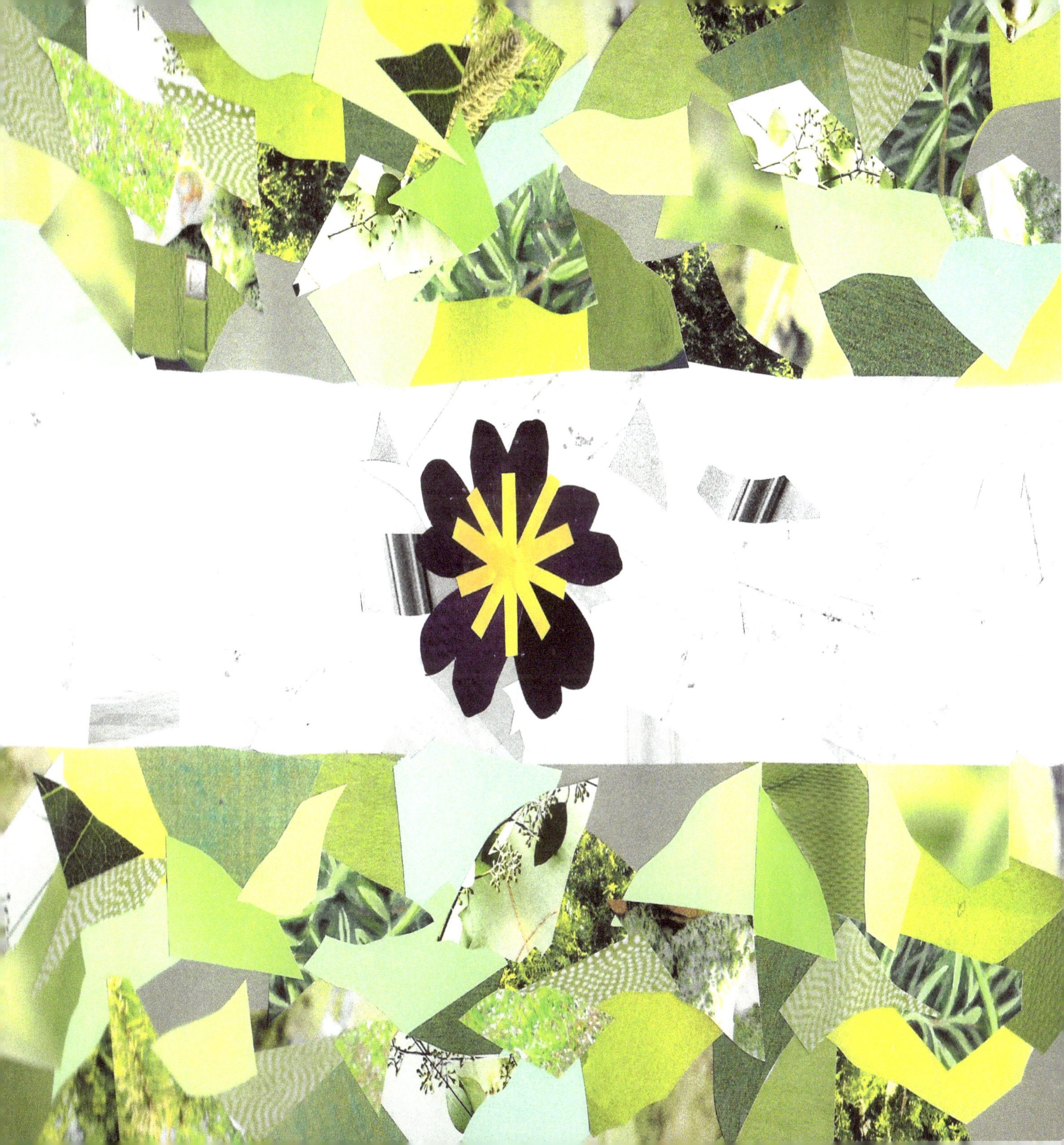

Autochoris/Aego

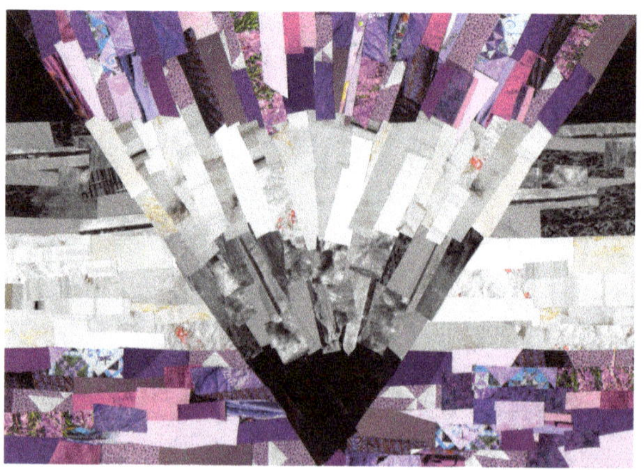

People who are Autochorissexual/Aegosexual or Autochorisromantic/Aegoromantic experience a disconnect between themselves and the object of their interest. They also may be people who are interested in a romantic or sexual relationship that is not connected to their attraction. These identities are on the aromantic and asexual spectrums.

These are people that probably do not experience the form of attract that they are interested in but want to pursue those relationships. Just because a person is one does not mean they identify as the other. They also may use other labels to more fully describe their identity and experiences.

The autochorissexual flag is made up of four strips of black, grey, white, and green. One top of those strips is a triangle made up of four strips that reverse the order of colors to purple, white, grey, and black. The autochorisromantic flag is similar except that it replaces purple with green.

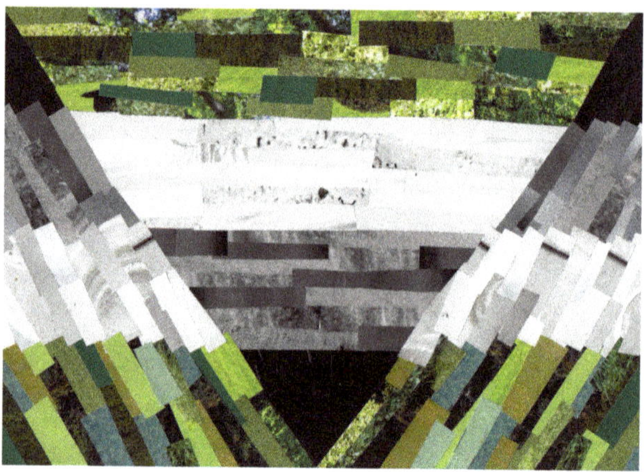

Cupio (formerly known as Kalos)

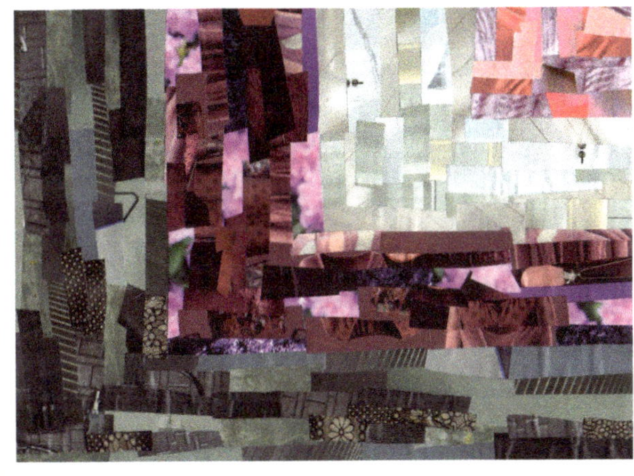

Someone who is Cupioromantic/cupiosexual does not experience the form of attraction they use a label for but still desires that kind of relationship. For example, someone who is cupiosexual may also identify as gay. However, they likely do not experience attraction for the same gender. They use the word gay and then cupiosexual to discuss how they want a gay relationship even though they do not experience attraction towards people of the same gender. Thus, they may not be sexually or romantically attracted to people but still want to have a relationship. Cupio is an excellent example of how actions do not necessarily equal attraction.

This identity falls along the asexual and aromantic spectrums because the person does not experience attraction despite their wish for a relationship.

There is any number of reasons a person may wish to enter a relationship beyond attraction, be that for companionship, children, a family, or fun.

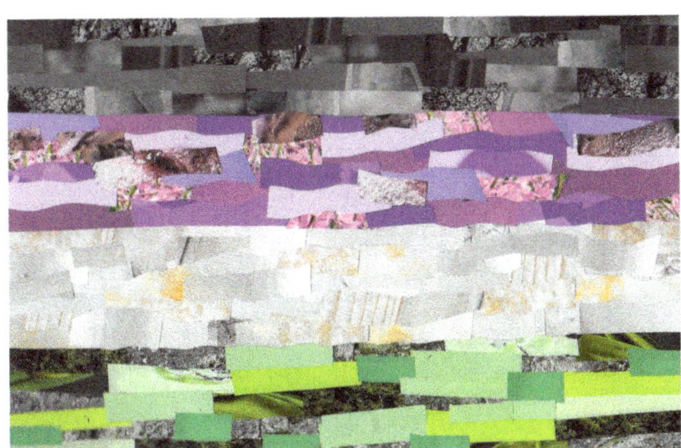

The cupio flag has several variations. The one pictured here with pink, white, purple, and grey stripes is the cupiosexual pride flag. The cupioromantic pride flag pictured is grey, purple, white, and black.

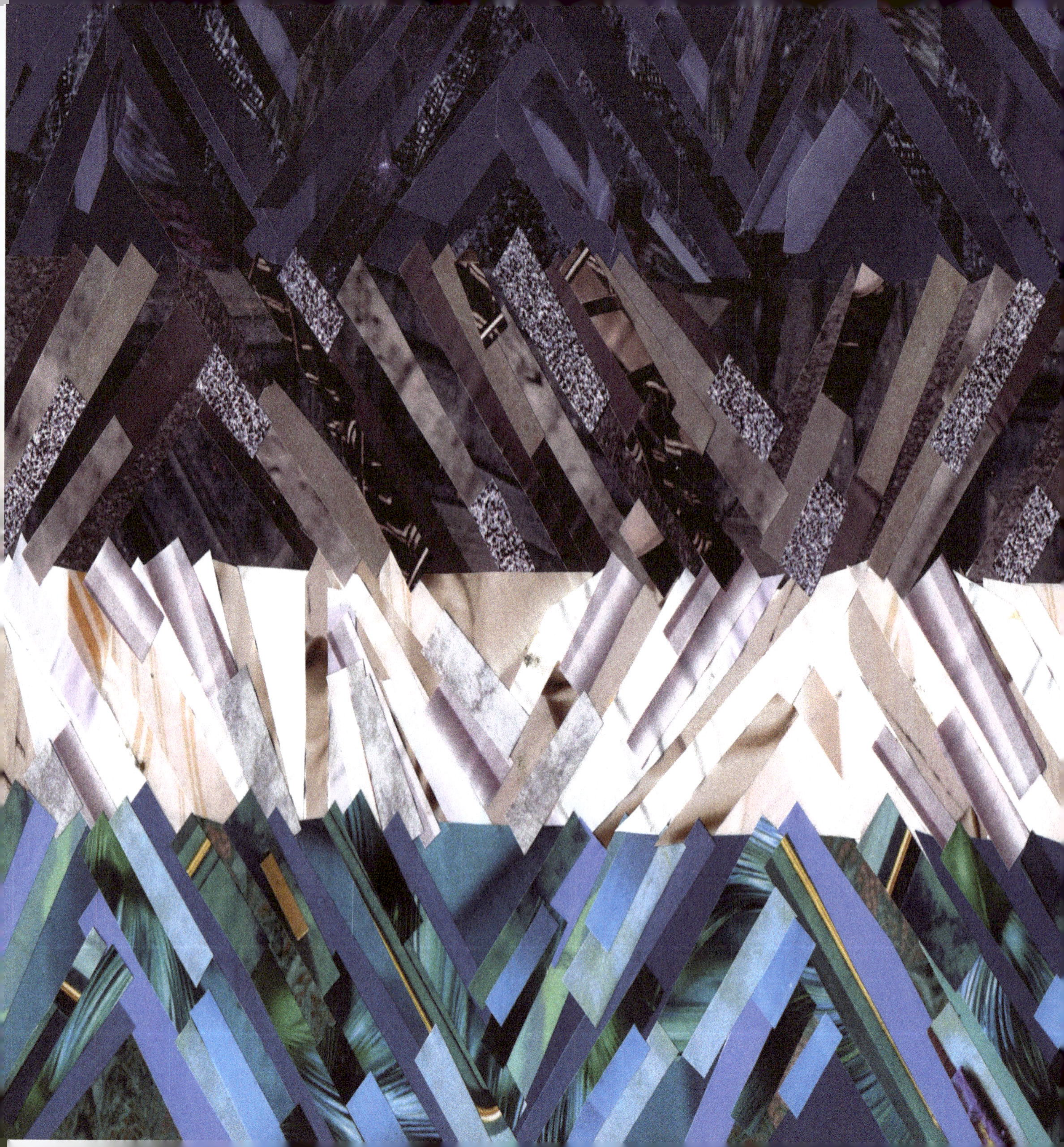

Oriented AroAce

Oriented Aromantic Asexual people are people who want to add another term to go with how they experience attraction, though not in a romantic and sexual nature. These come in the form of platonic attraction, sensual attraction, aesthetic attraction, alterous attraction, queerplatonic attraction, or a combination of these.

Thus, they usually pair it with another word like gay, bi, pan, or some other label to talk about this form of tertiary attraction outside of the sexual and romantic attractions. Generally, this term is used by people who fully identify as aromantic and asexual but wish to be more specific and complete in defining other forms attraction.

The flag is four stripes of dark blue, grey, white, and a teal-ish green.

Angled AroAce

Angled AroAce people is when someone is both on the aromantic and asexual spectrum, though not necessarily just aromantic and asexual. This means they could be demi or grey or some other identity on the aromantic and asexual spectrums. Thus, they experience some other form of romantic or sexual attraction combined with their aroace identity.

This can be paired with any other orientation to describe someone's identity and the person will likely use one or two of the aromantic or asexual spectrum identities with something like bi, pan, gay, or any other descriptor of who they experience attraction to.

Angled aroaces are different from oriented aroaces in the fact that angled aroaces do experience some level of romantic or sexual attraction, no matter how rare.

The angled aroace flag is made up of five stripes that are a dark yellow to black gradient.

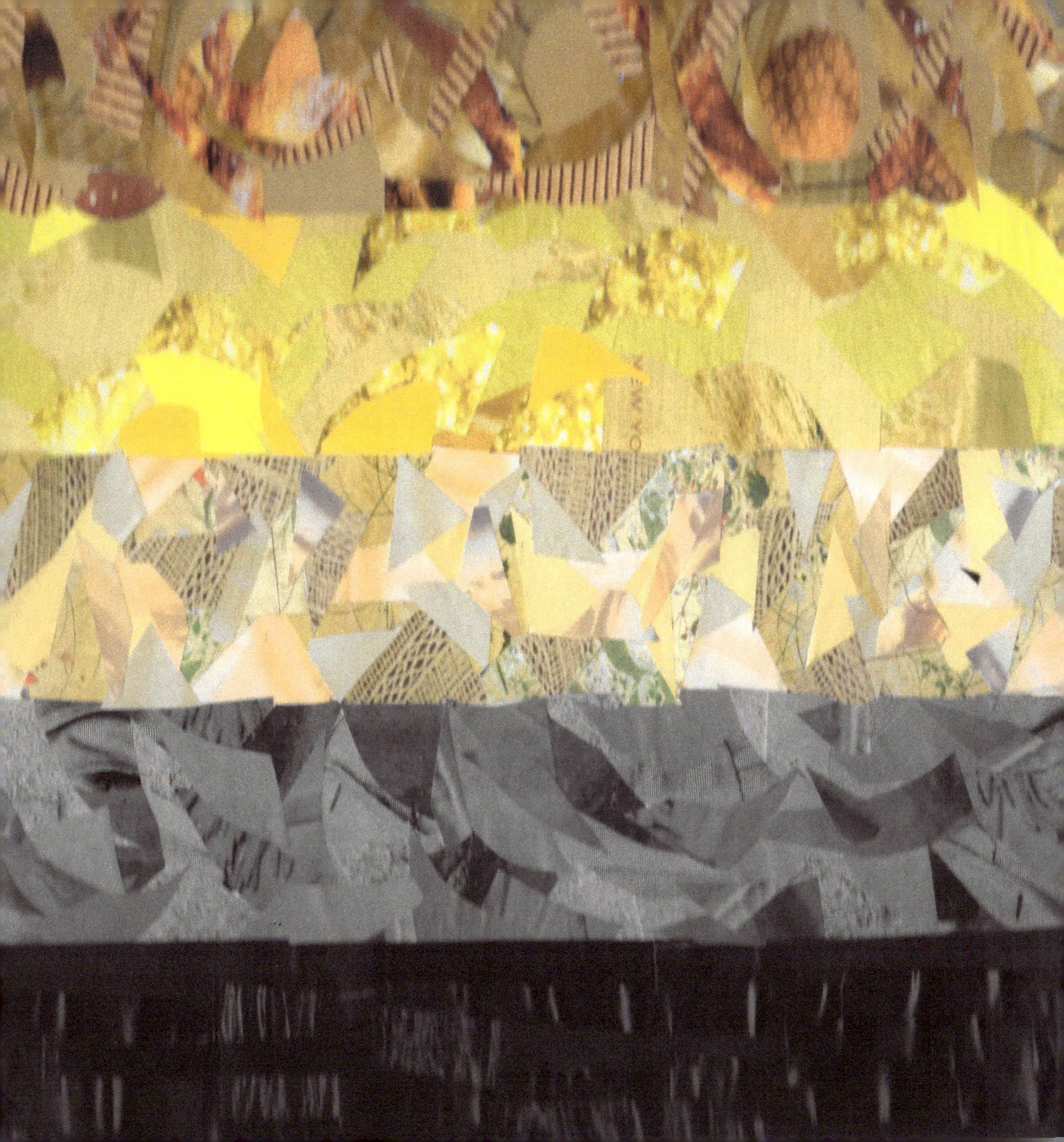

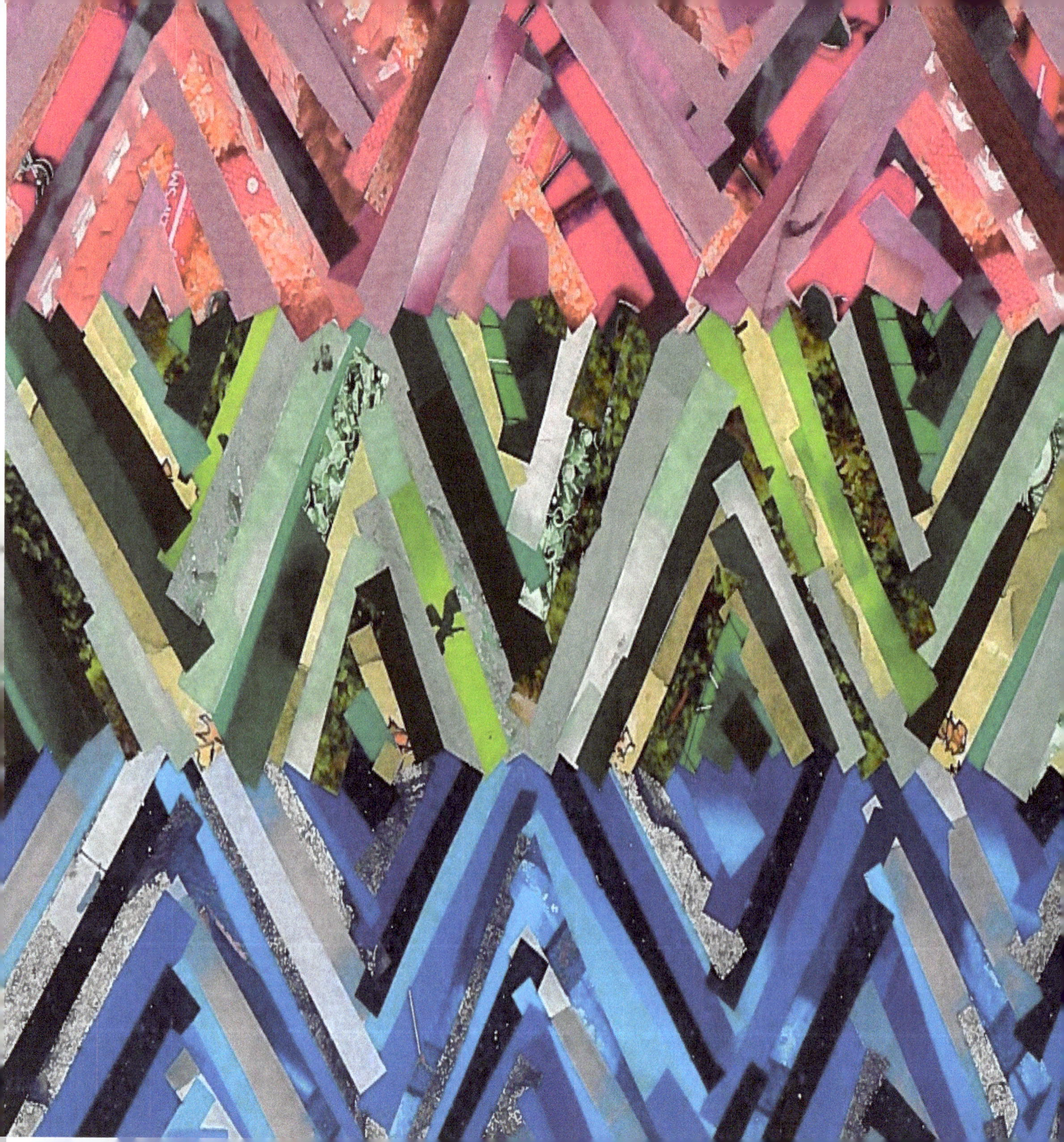

Poly

(not polyamorous, that's later)

Polysexual and polyromantic people are not to be confused for polyamorous people. The polysexual orientation is much like being bi or pan in that they are attracted to more than one gender.

Importantly, they are not necessarily attracted to all genders, just more than one gender. This makes it different than orientations like omni.

Often, this is just something people feel more at home identifying with rather than other options like bi or pan.

The polysexual/polyromantic pride flag is made up of three stripes of pink, green, and blue.

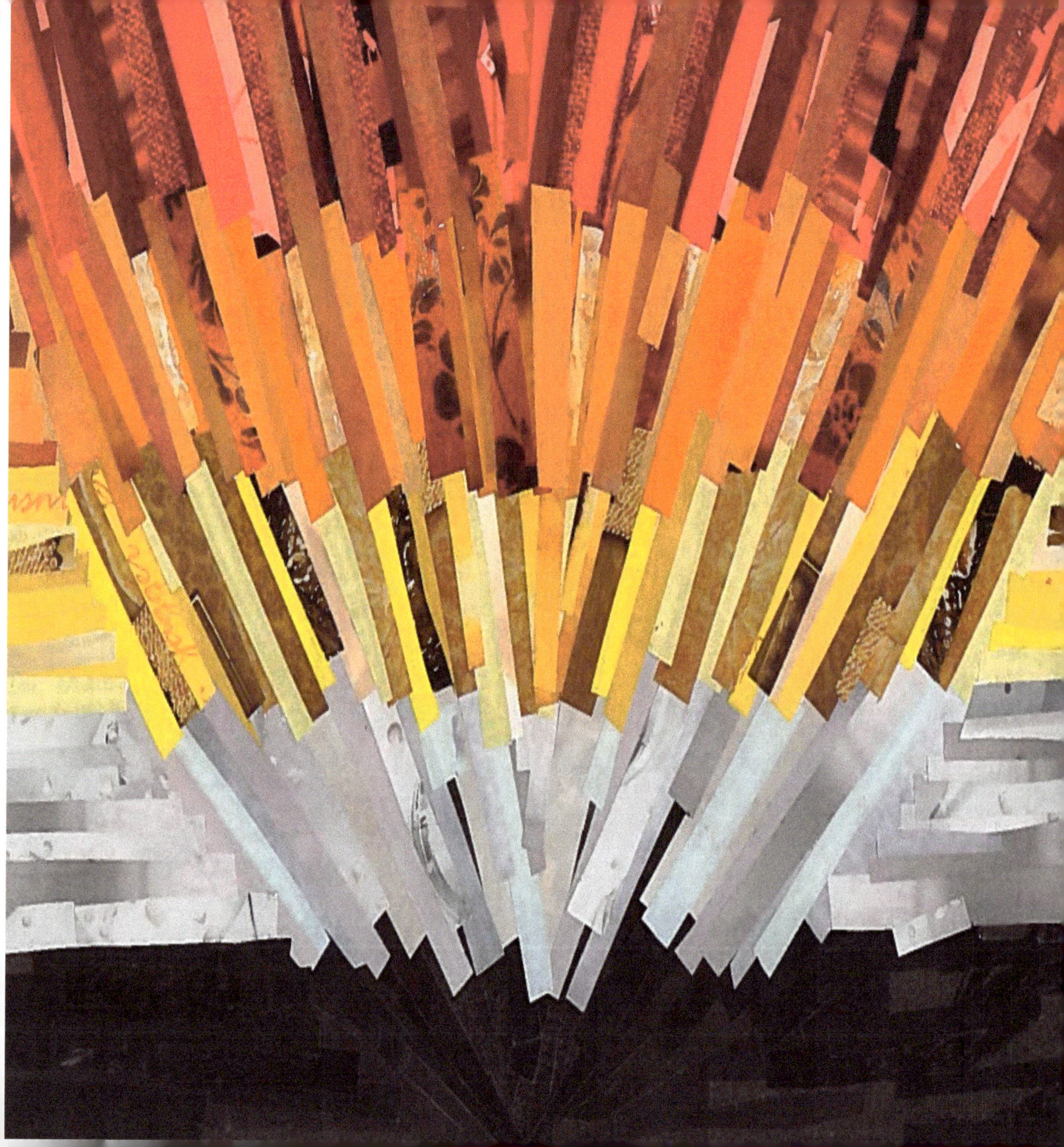

Lithromantic (Akioromantic or Apromantic)

Lithromantic falls on the spectrum between aromantic and alloromantic. Someone who is lithromantic enjoys the idea of a romantic relationship in theory but may lose interest quickly once they realize that is reciprocated. Thus, they tend to prefer the idea of romance but not necessarily in their own lives.

This can look like someone who fantasizes about a romantic relationship but freezes up or loses any form of attraction the moment it is returned.

There are other pride flag designs for this orientation. The one pictured is the most commonly seen. It is five stripes of red, orange, yellow, white, and black.

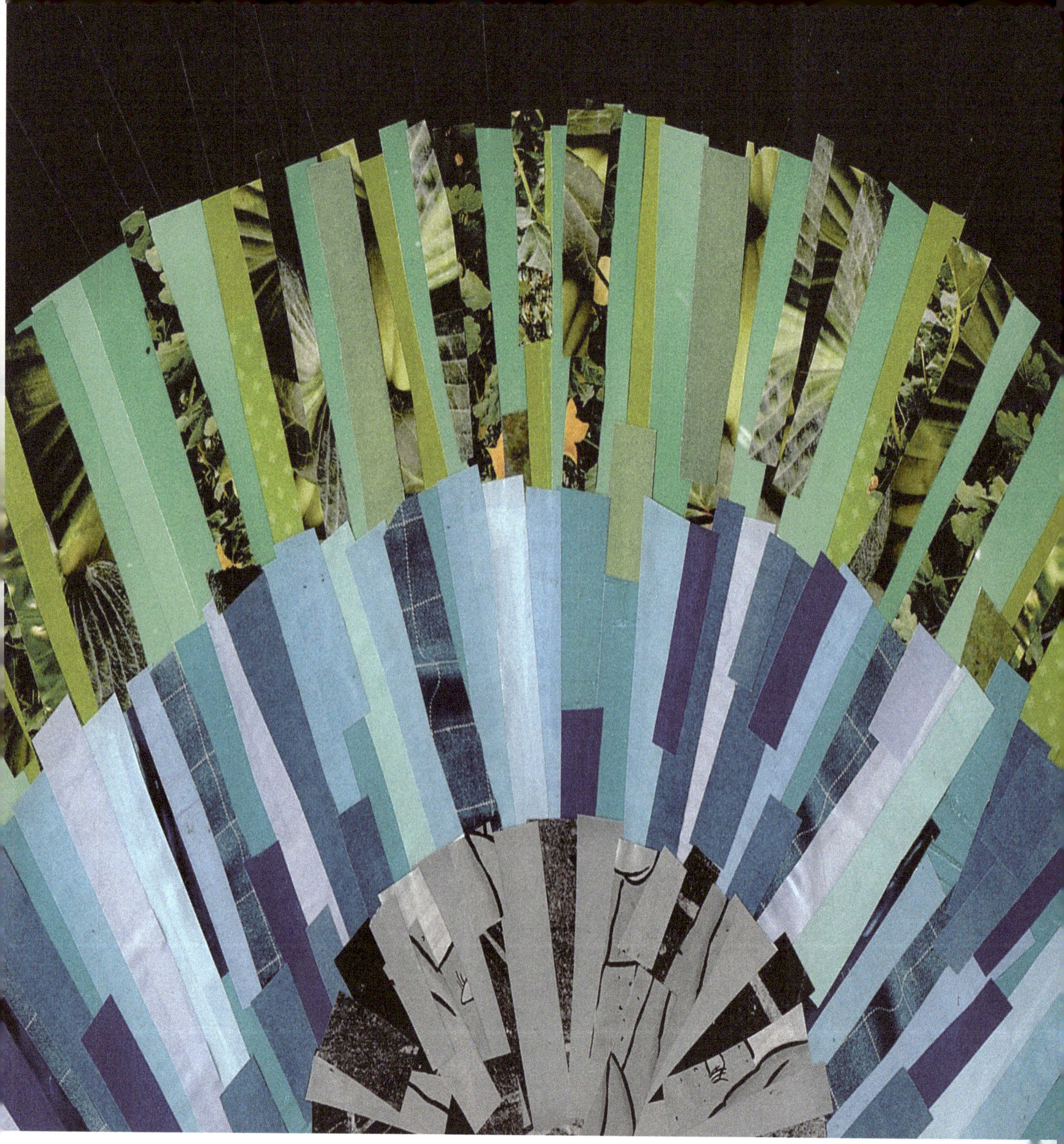

Quoiromantic

Quoiromantic is based off the French word for 'what' and you can tell when you look at it's definition. Being quoiromantic can mean two things: not understanding or misidentifying romantic attraction or feeling like that attraction is so far away that it is inaccessible or nonsensical. This is also sometimes referred to as WTFromantic in reference to romantic attraction making absolutely not sense, so wtf?

This tends to fall along the aromantic spectrum as someone who does not quite experience romantic attraction or is unable to identify romantic attraction.

There are a few flag variations for this orientation. The one pictured here is four stripes of black, green, blue, and grey.

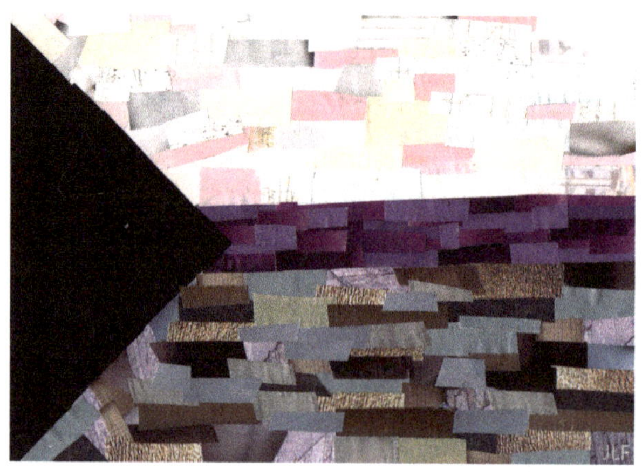

Demisexual/Demiromantic/ Demirose

Demisexual and demiromantic are steps between the alloromantic/allosexuals and aromantic/asexuals. Someone who identifies as demi can only experience that form of attraction after they have formed a strong emotional bond with someone, which means they likely won't experience attraction towards just anyone. That does not mean they will become attracted to anyone that they know well, just that they must know someone well before they can be attracted to them.

This is different from the average person who might only pursue a relationship with someone they know well but are attracted to people generally regardless of how much they know them.

These orientations can be combined with any other identity or can be used on their own. That is completely up to the person using the term and does not necessarily apply to other aspects of their orientation.

Demirose is the orientation that combines both of demisexual and demiromantic. That means that the person would identity as both.

The demisexual, demiromantic, and demirose flags are very similar. All three have a black triangle on the left with a white stripe on top and a grey stripe on bottom. The only difference is that the demisexual flag has a purple stripe in the middle, the demiromantic flag has a green strip in the middle, and the demirose flag has a navy stripe in the middle.

Well Known Demi Person: Alex Kazemi (author).

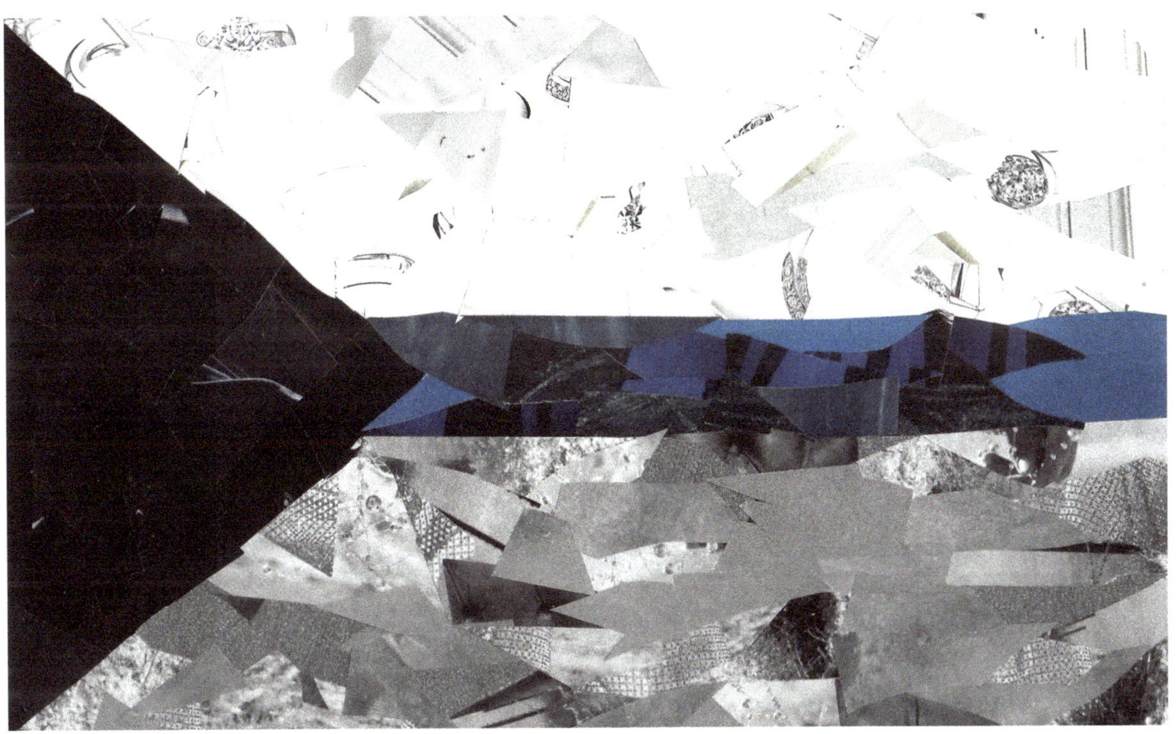

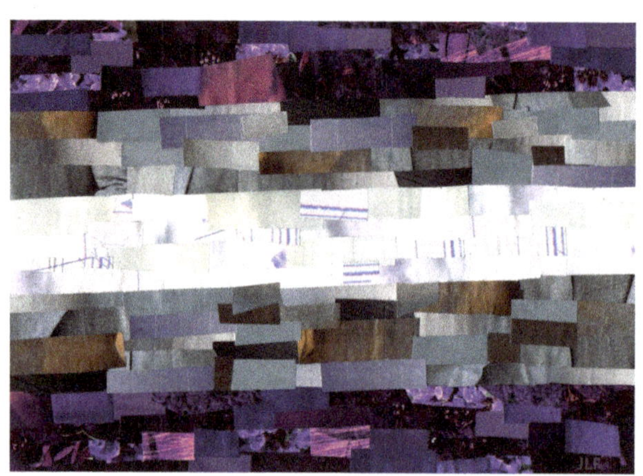

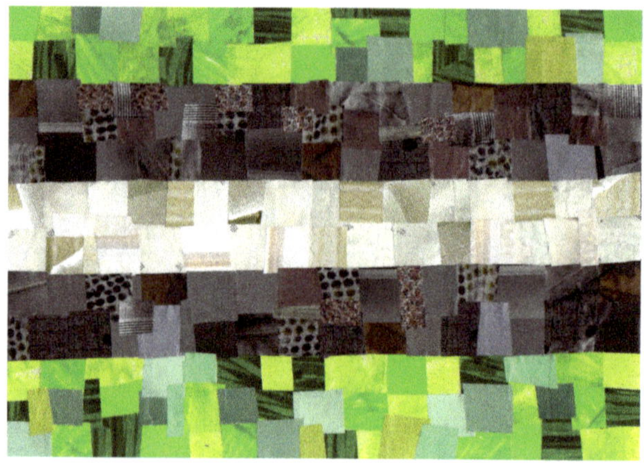

Grey

Greysexual and Greyromantic are other steps between the alloromantic/allosexuals and aromantic/asexuals. People who experience attraction this way often feel their attraction either incredibly infrequently or very weakly to the point that they do not identify as alloromantic or allosexual.

These orientations can be combined with any other identity or can be used on their own. That is completely up to the person using the term. Identifying as greyromantic does not necessarily mean that a person identifies as greysexual and vice versa.

The greysexual flag is five stripes of purple, grey, white, grey, and purple. The greyromantic flag is five stripes of green, grey, white, grey, and green.

Abrosexual

Abrosexual means that someone experiences different levels of attraction over time. This is a bit like genderfluid in the sense that the person's identity is more fluid than others and takes on a consistently shifting nature that the person wants to label as their whole identity. However, this applies to a person's sexuality rather than their gender.

This could be a shift in how much a person is attracted to people ranging from some level of asexual to allosexual or something else.

The abrosexual flag is made up of five stripes of dark green, light green, white, red, and a dark red.

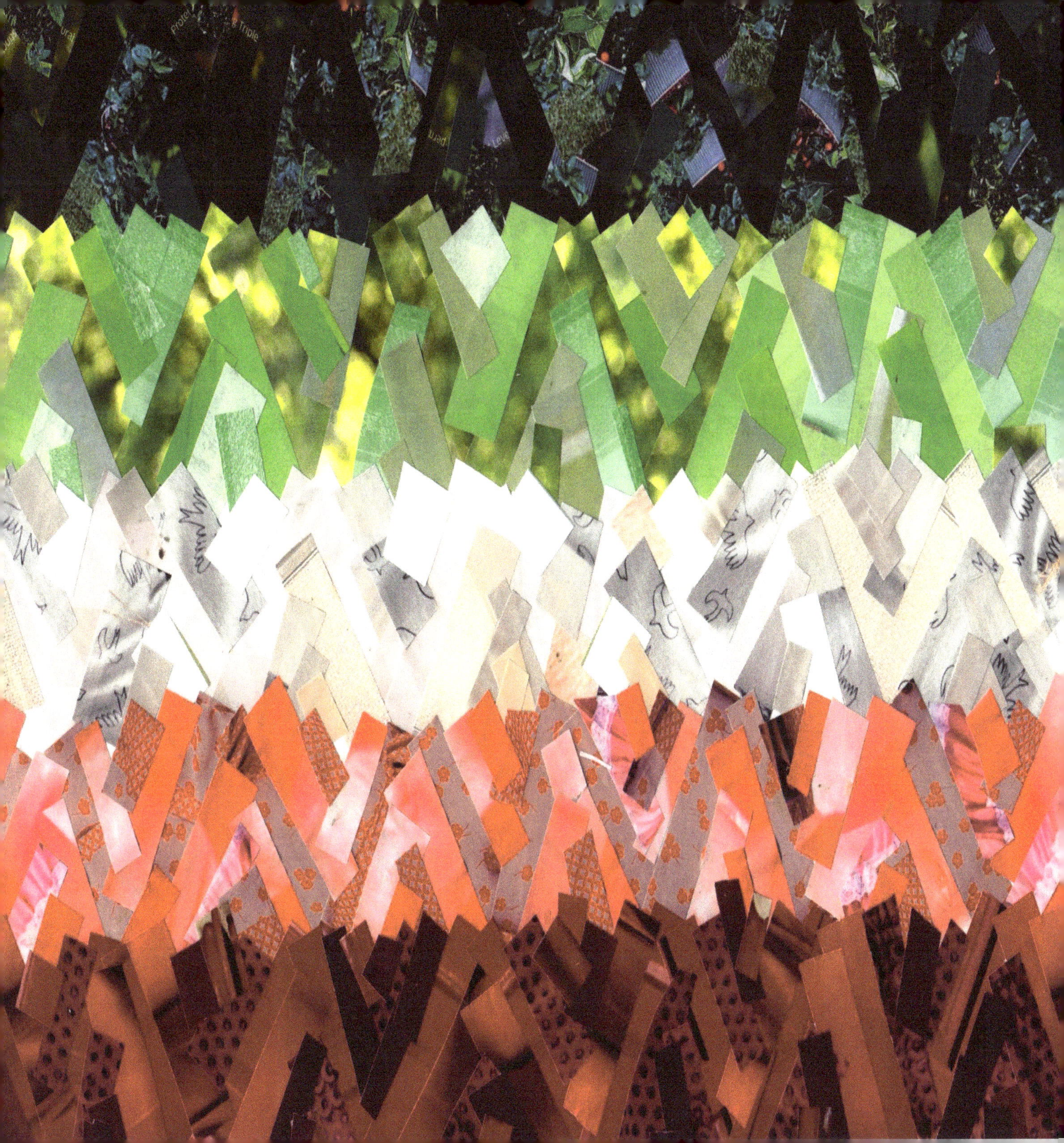

Omni

Omnisexual and omniromantic people are characterized by being attracted to all genders. Unlike pansexual, gender is more likely to play a role in the person's attraction here but they are still attracted to all genders.

This is another version of multi-gender attraction and is an identity that many find comfort and recognition in. This is probably the most all encompassing of multigender attraction labels with omni meaning all rather than just two or several.

The omni pride flag is five stripes of light pink, pink, dark blue, blue, and light blue.

Well Known Fictional Omni Person: Captain Jack Harkness (Doctor Who character).

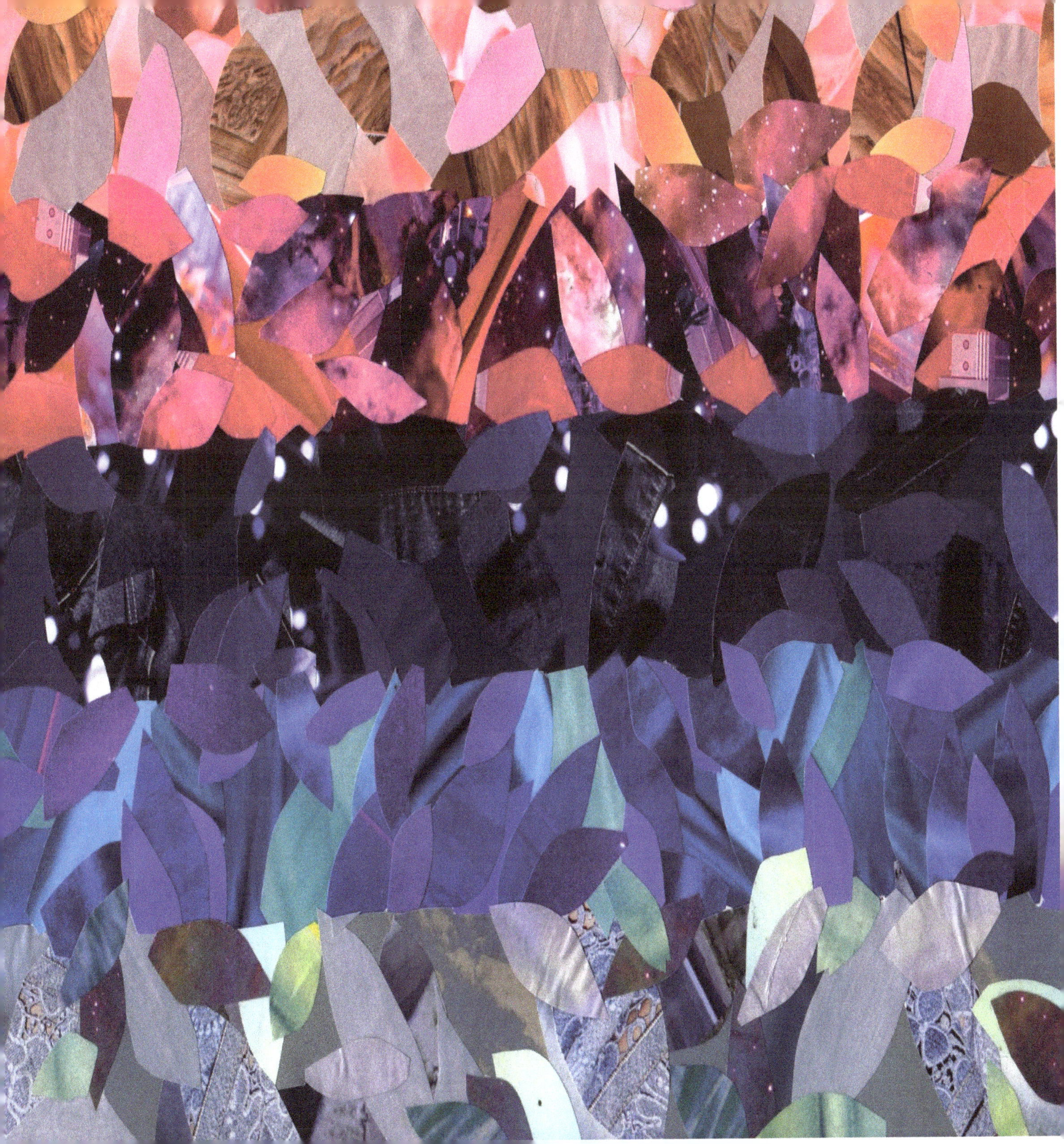

Trixic or Orbisian

Trixic people are nonbinary people who are attracted to women. It can be abbreviated to NBLW which means nonbinary loving women. This is not an exclusive identity and can be used with other terms depending on the person using it.

As we have seen, the nonbinary identity is as broad as romantic and sexual orientations. Thus, there are many ways someone may use this term depending on their gender identity as well as their sexual and romantic orientations.

The trixic pride flag made up of five strips that is a gradient from purple to orange with pink in the middle. There are other trixic pride flags including one that mimics the styles of sapphic and achillean flags with a flower in the middle.

Well Known Potentially Trixic Person: Cara Jocelyn Delevingne is a genderfluid actor and singer who is bisexual/pansexual, so she could be trixic.

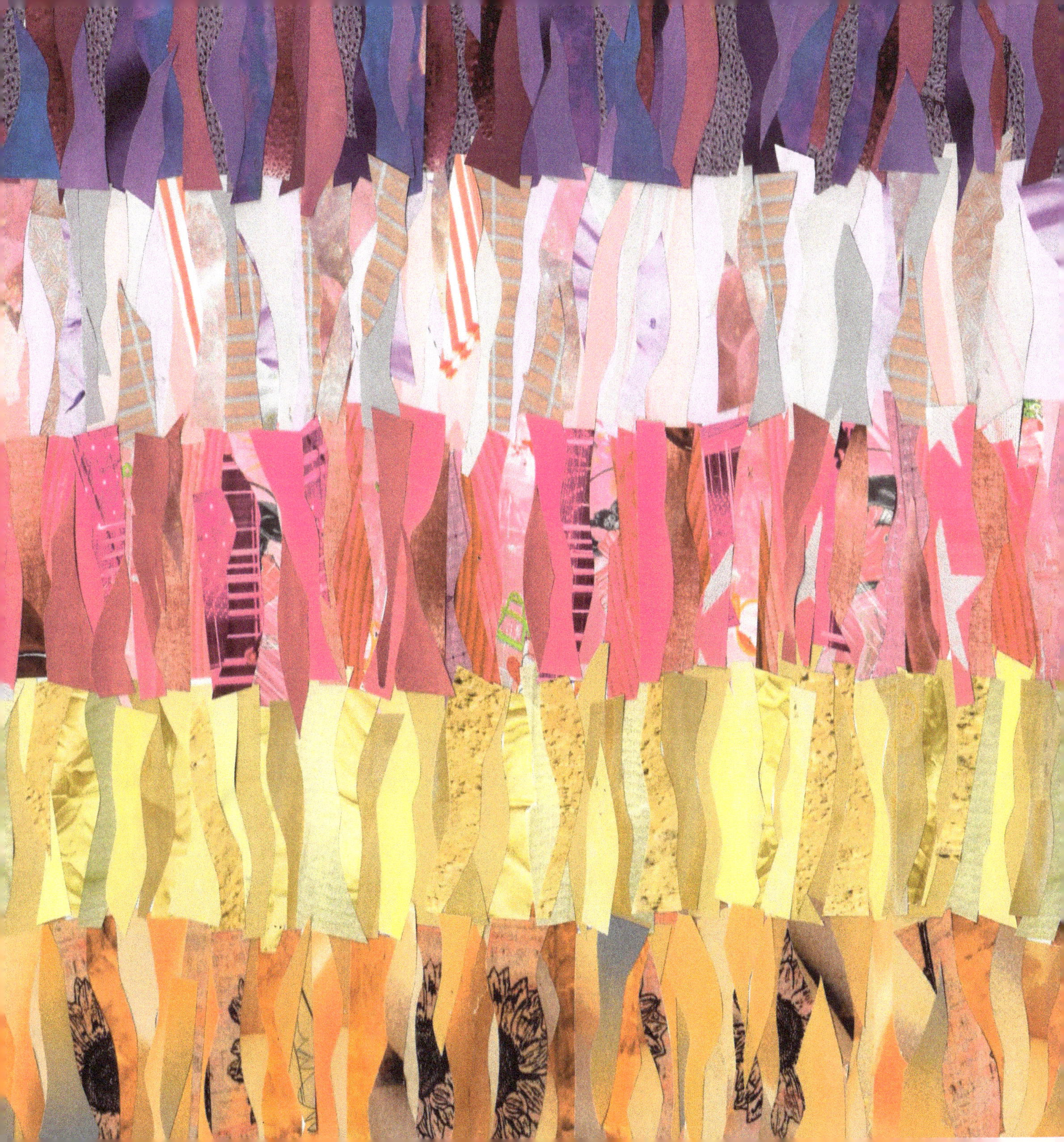

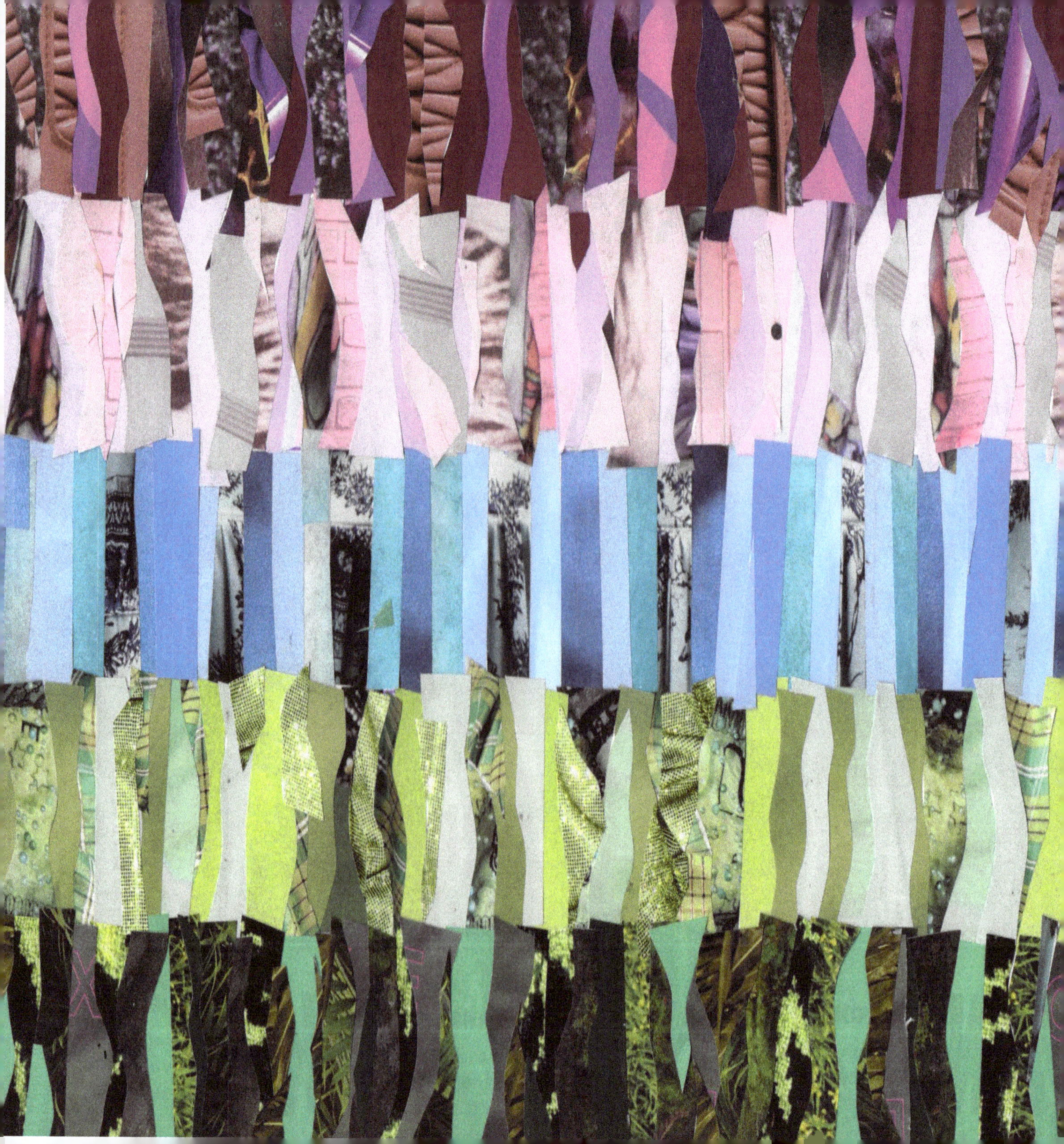

Toric or Quadrisian

Someone who is Toric is a nonbinary person who is attracted to men. It can be abbreviated to NBLM which means nonbinary loving men.

As we have seen with trixic, toric, and other identities, the nonbinary identity is as broad as romantic and sexual orientations. Thus, there are many ways someone may use this term depending on their gender identity as well as their sexual and romantic orientations.

The toric pride flag is five stripes of purple, light purple, blue, light green, and green. There are other iterations, but this is generally the most recognized.

Well Known Potentially Toric Person: Jonathan Van Ness from Queer Eye is a non-binary person who is attraction to men, so he could be toric.

Enbian or Owtic

Enbian means that someone is a nonbinary person attracted to other nonbinary people. This can be an exclusive identity in that is the other people they feel attraction to or be paired with any other sexual or romantic orientation. This can be shorted to NBLNB which stands for nonbinary loving nonbinary.

Like trixic and toric, enbian people can pair this label with other label of attraction and other gender identities.

The enbian pride flag pictured here is made up of five stripes that are orange, light orange, white, green, and dark green. However, this is not the most common pride flag. The most common one is a gradient of a dark purple to a light purple with a yellow crest of a moon in the center. However, purple in magazines is difficult to find and this was a commonly used alternative.

Well Known Potentially Enbian Person: Gigi Raven Wilbur is an activist who was one of the founders of "Celebrate Bisexuality Day" and is bi or pan, so he could be considered enbian.

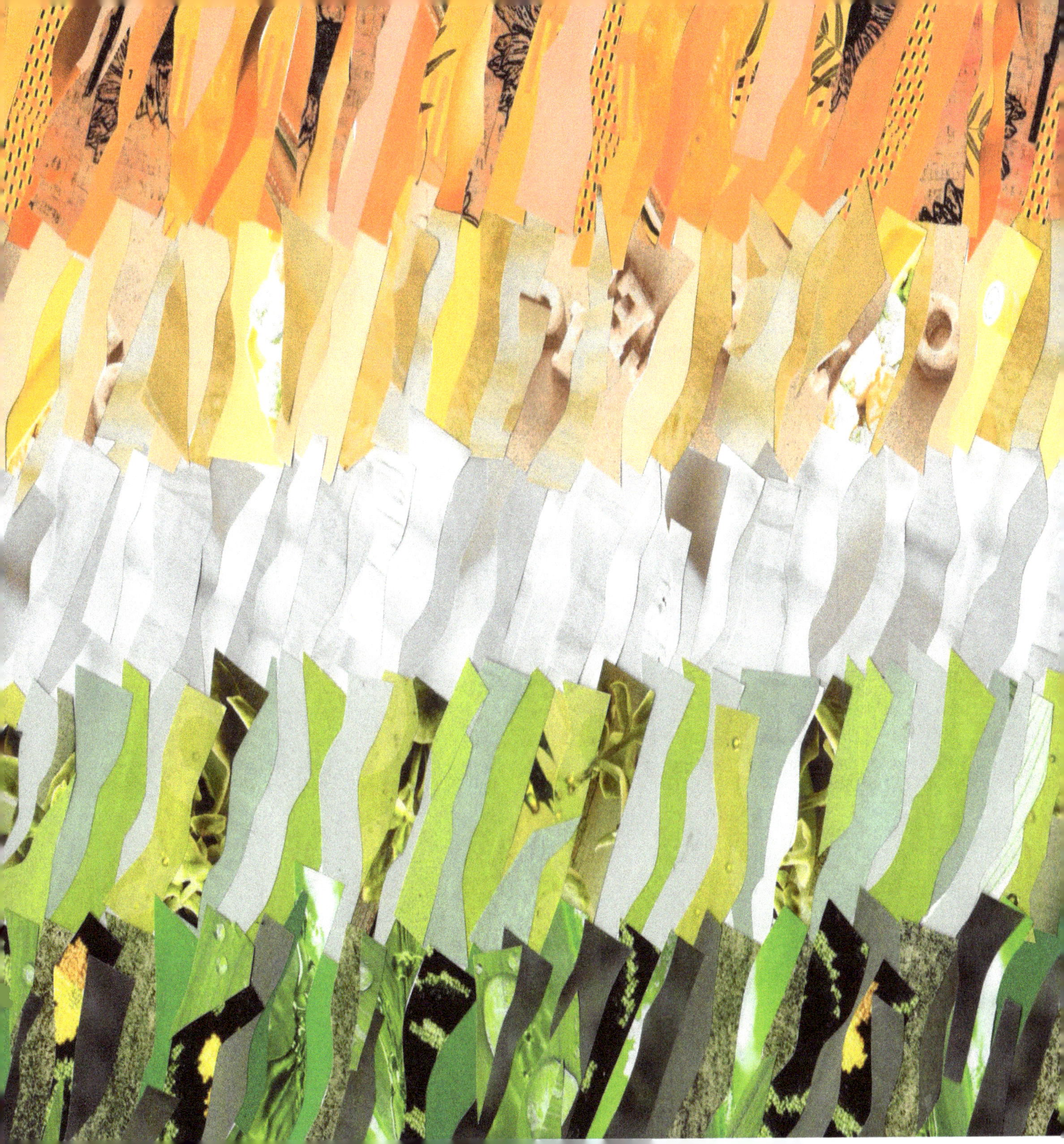

Idemromantic

Idemromantic is on the aromantic spectrum and falls into a subcategory of quoiromantic. People who are idemromantic experience romantic and platonic attraction but cannot differentiate between them internally and rather have to use external factors.

With these indistinguishable internal attractions, the person may feel very similarly for a best friend as they would a romantic partner. External factors rather than internal attraction would dictate how the idemromantic person would approach the relationship and person.

Much like other aromantic identities, this can be paired with any other orientation to better explain how a person experiences attraction.

The idemromantic flag is made up of four stripes of black, green, white, and red.

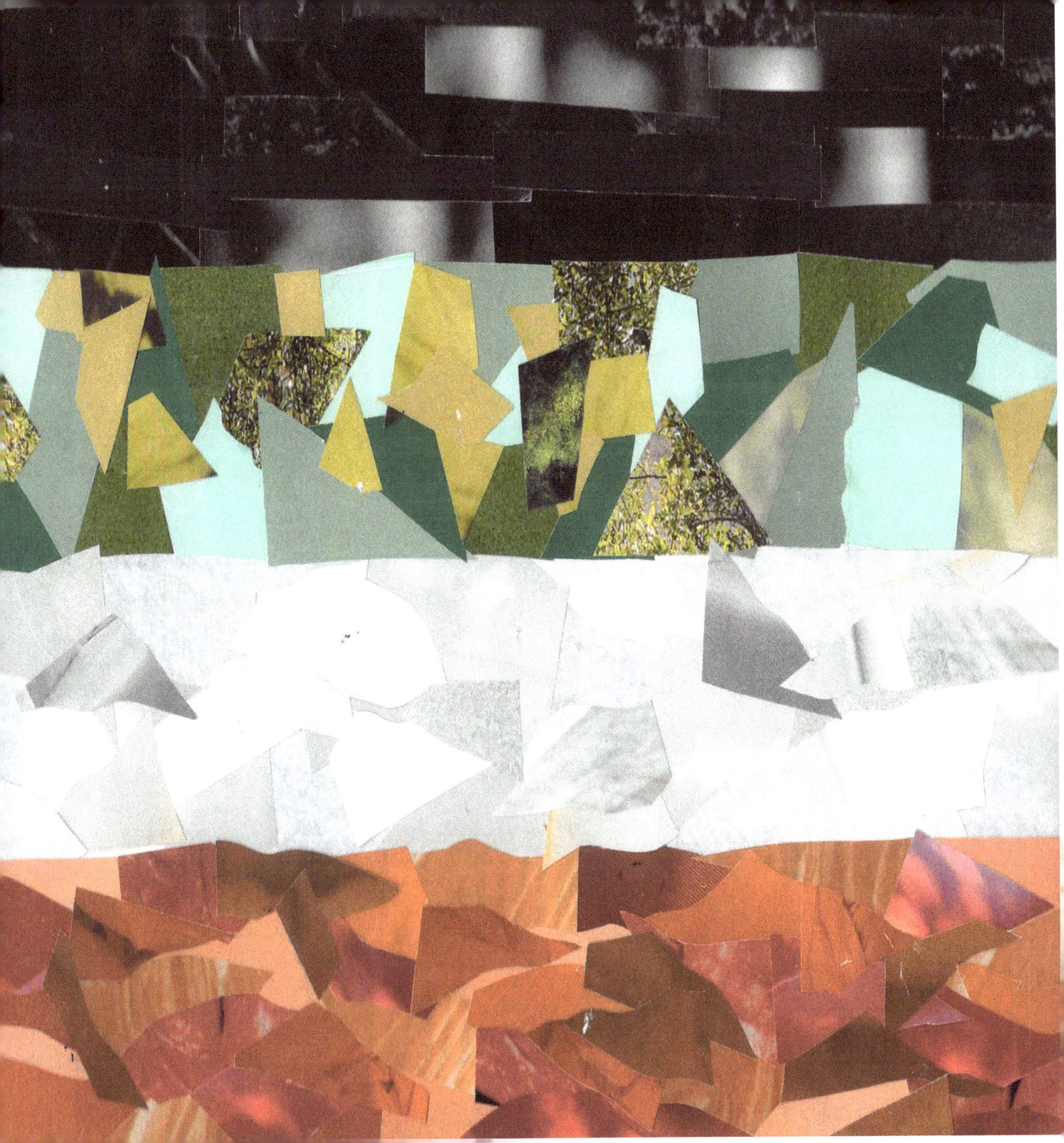

Recipro

Reciprosexual/Reciproromantic people are on the aromantic and asexual spectrums. People who use this label do not experience attraction until they know someone else is attracted to them. This does not mean that they necessarily will be interested in just anyone who is attracted to them but rather that the other person's attraction to them is a necessary factor to even have a chance at returning said attraction.

This is different from the nerves that some people experience when they experience attraction and feel more at home once they know their feelings in return. After all, the attraction for non-reciprosexual/reciproromantic people existed without knowing the other person was attracted to them.

Anyone who uses these labels can use other labels to help describe what genders they may be attracted to.

The flag for reciprosexual is five stripes of pink, light pink, purple, white and black. Reciproromantic is five stripes of pink, light, green, white, and black.

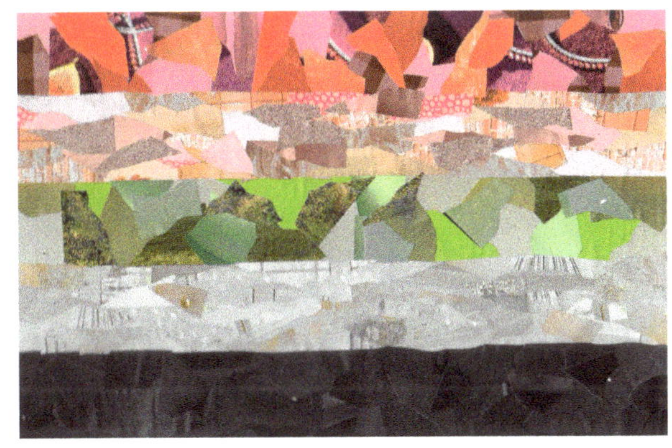

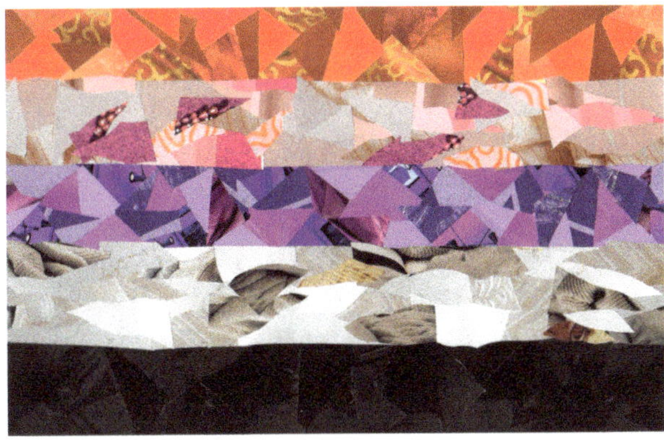

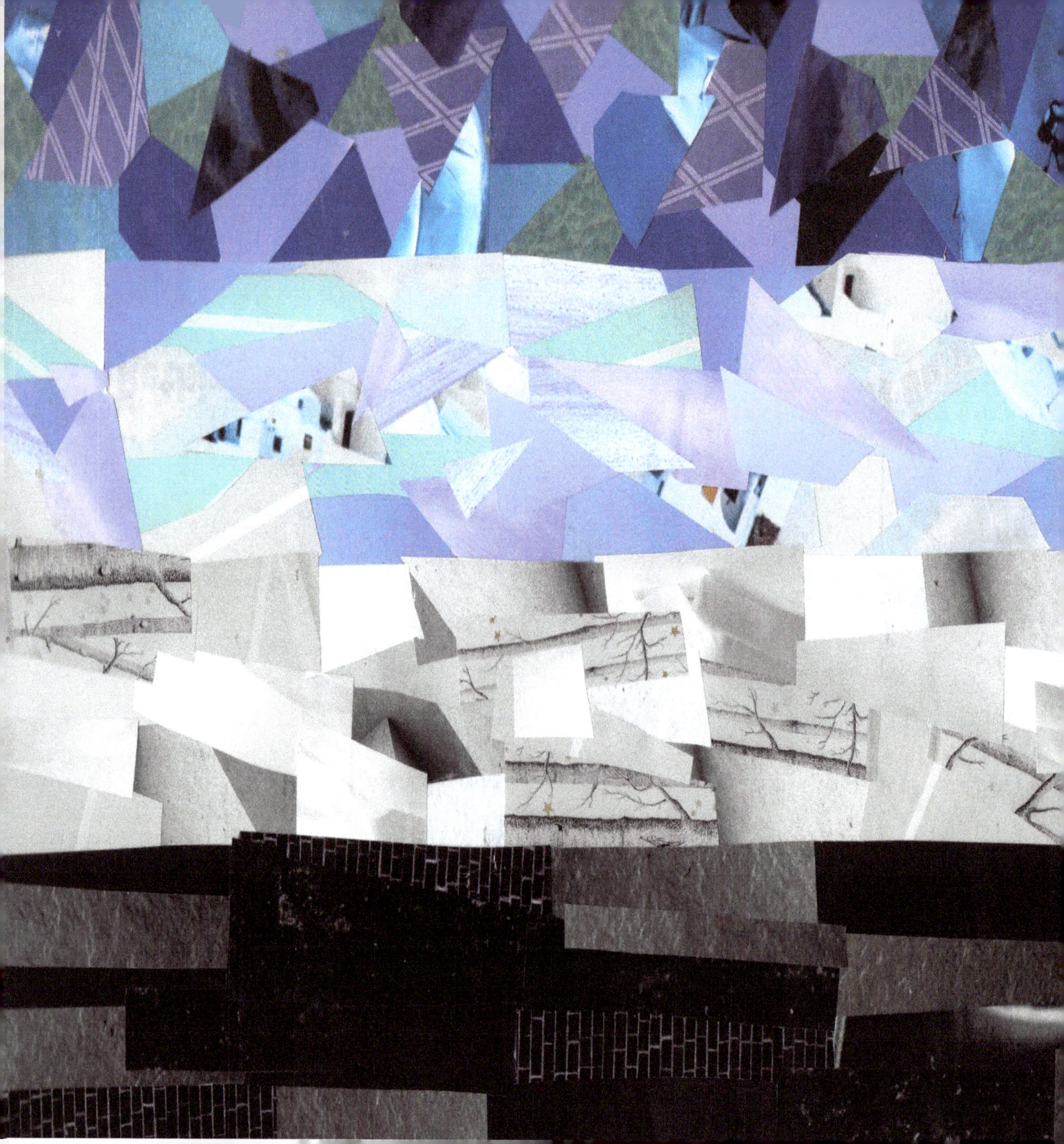

Fray

Fraysexual/Frayromantic people are nearly the opposite of demisexual/demiromantic people in that they only experience attraction to people they do not know well. This doesn't mean they will lose sensual or platonic attraction, so fraysexual/frayromantic people may still pursue relationships after the attraction goes away.

This identity is on the aromantic and asexual spectrums. Thus, like other identities on this spectrum, fray people may identify with other labels as well and often pair those labels together to better describe their experiences.

The fraysexual flag is the one pictured here. It is four stripes of dark blue, light blue, white, and black.

Romo Aro

A person who is a romantic aromantic (or Romo Aro) is someone who falls under the aromantic umbrella while also experiencing some form of romantic attraction or desire for a romantic relationship.

People who opt to identify as romo aro could be greyromantic, demiromantic, or a number of orientations we've yet to discuss like lovequeer. They also may be someone who desires a romantic relationship without actually experiencing any attraction.

The romantic aromantic pride flag is made up of seven strips, four of equal size and three in the middle that split up what would have been the third stripe. In order, the flag is dark green, light green, pink, white, pink, grey, and black.

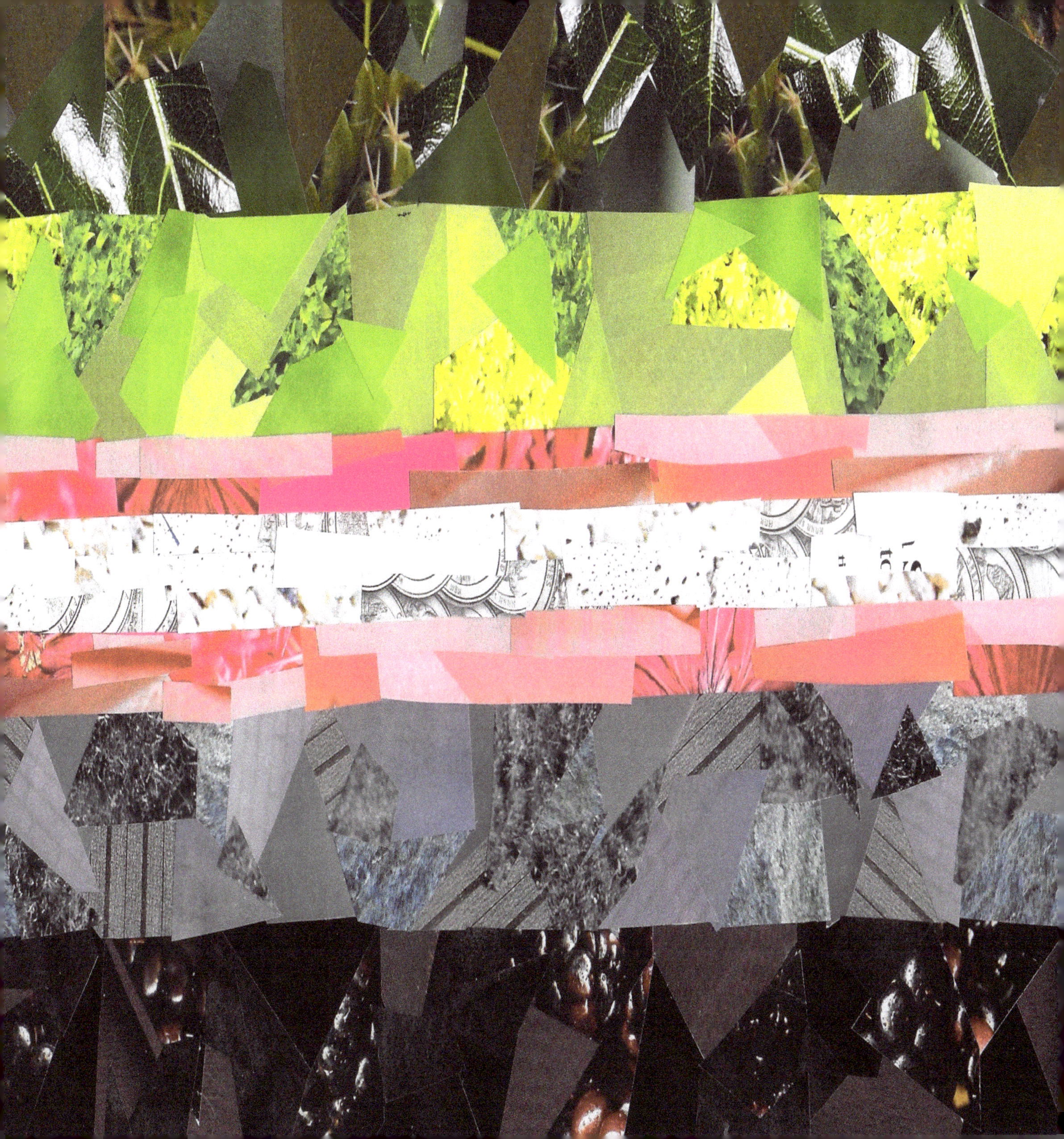

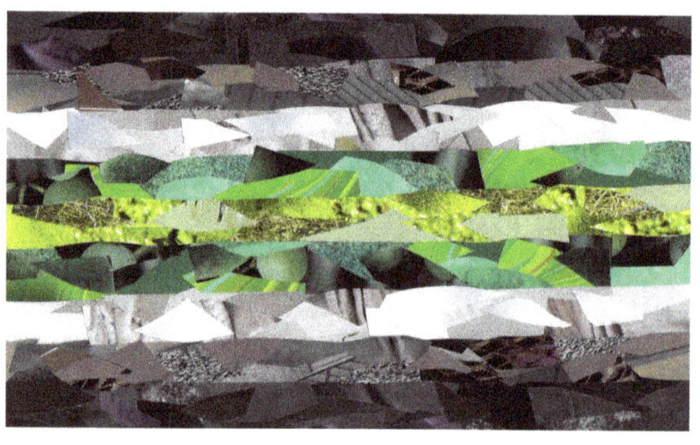

Loveless Aromantic

A Loveless Aromantic person is someone on the aromantic spectrum who feels disconnected from love. Importantly, someone who is aromantic will not necessarily identify as loveless. This is a subsection of the community, much like demiromantic or greyromantic.

Some ways a loveless aromantic has described their experiences include feeling uncomfortable with love as a concept, not finding love important to their lives, or thinking they don't experience love but rather only compassion, appreciate, or respect for others.

The loveless aromantic pride flag is made up on nine equal sized stripes which repeat around the center stripe. Working from the outward strip inwards, both sides are black, grey, white, and dark green before reaching the center, light green stripe.

Heartless Aromantic

A Heartless Aromantic person also feels separated from any form of love or romance. This could be for any number of reasons like feeling disconnected to the idea of love and romance.

Heartless aromantics can sometimes feel rejected by society's standards of relationships which leads them to embrace this identity. Others feel uncomfortable with the idea of conforming to these standards, though do not necessarily feel rejected by others.

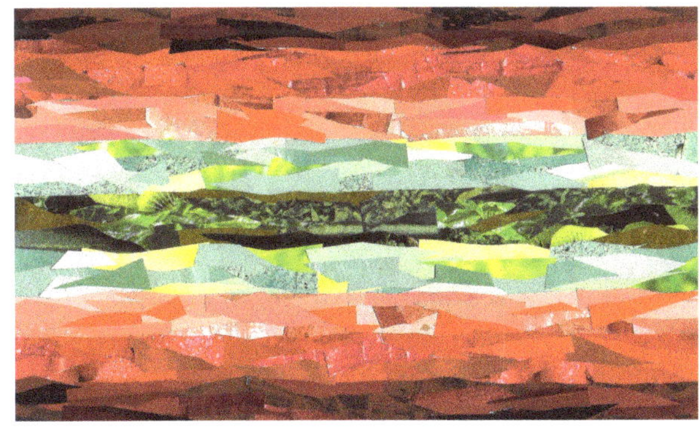

Some people identify as heartless aromantic to reclaim the word "heartless". This is because aromantics can often be called heartless for not experiencing romantic attraction, and some find power and self-acceptance in making that a specific part of their identity.

The heartless aro pride flag is made up of nine strips which are the same on either side before meeting in the middle. These stripes from the outside working in are dark red, red, light red, light green, and meet in the middle with a dark green stripe.

Love Integral Aromantic

On the other hand, some aromantics identify as Love Integral. Love for these people is at the center of one's identity and 'integral' to how they move through the world.

There are many different kinds of love that a person could value here outside of only romantic love. Whether platonic, familial, or another form of love, love integral aromantics find it to be vital to how they interact with people, themselves, and the world.

The love integral aromantic pride flag has four strips with a heart in the middle. The strips are blue, white, green, and white. The heart is in the middle of the pride flag. It is a blue heart that is outlined in white with green and white chevrons pointing upwards in the middle of it.

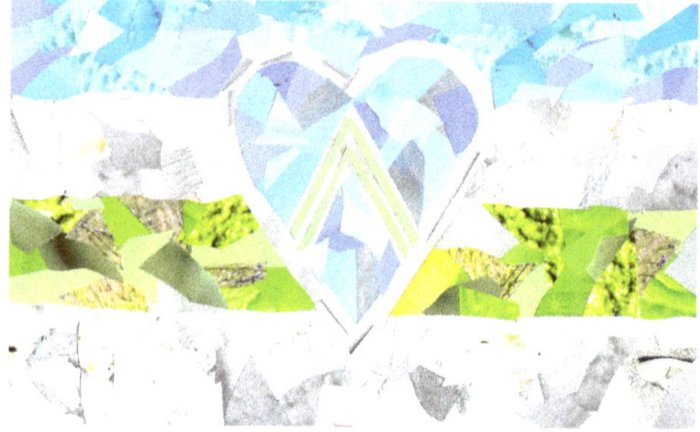

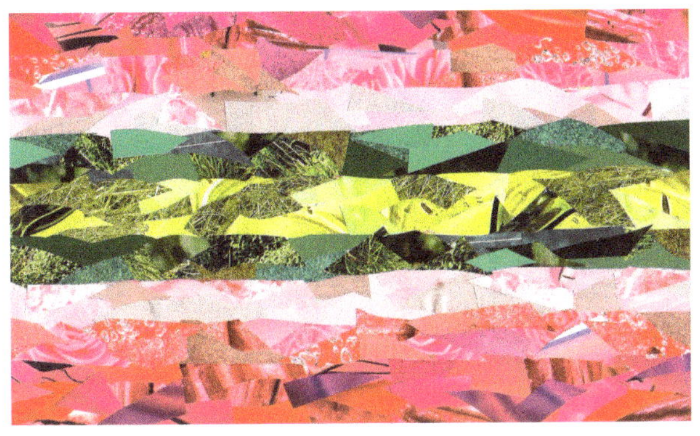

AroLovic

Arolovic, or aromantic lovic, is a similar identity to love integral aromantics. This is also for aromantic people who feel that love is an important part of their identity.

The idea of love can be important for any number of reasons, like discussed before. Love not only for people but also for objects, concepts, and the world around them can be vital for how people move through the world, especially arolovic people.

The arolovic pride flag is nine stripes that repeat on either side of the middle stripe. Working from the most outward stripe, each side is dark pink, pink, light pink, and green before meeting in the middle at a light green stripe.

Lovequeer

Lovequeer people fully reject the concept of love as it is usually applied to romantic relationships. Instead, lovequeer people take that word and redefine it for themselves.

People who are lovequeer focus more on types of love that society may ignore as a whole. This can be focusing not only on the family and friends that they love but also loving one's pets or other beings in their lives. Lovequeer is rejection of the idea that a person has to be in a romantic relationship to be happy.

The lovequeer flag is made up on nine stripes that are the same on either side before meeting at the middle stripe. From the outside to the middle, both sides are pink, yellow, light yellow, and grey before meeting in the middle with a white stripe.

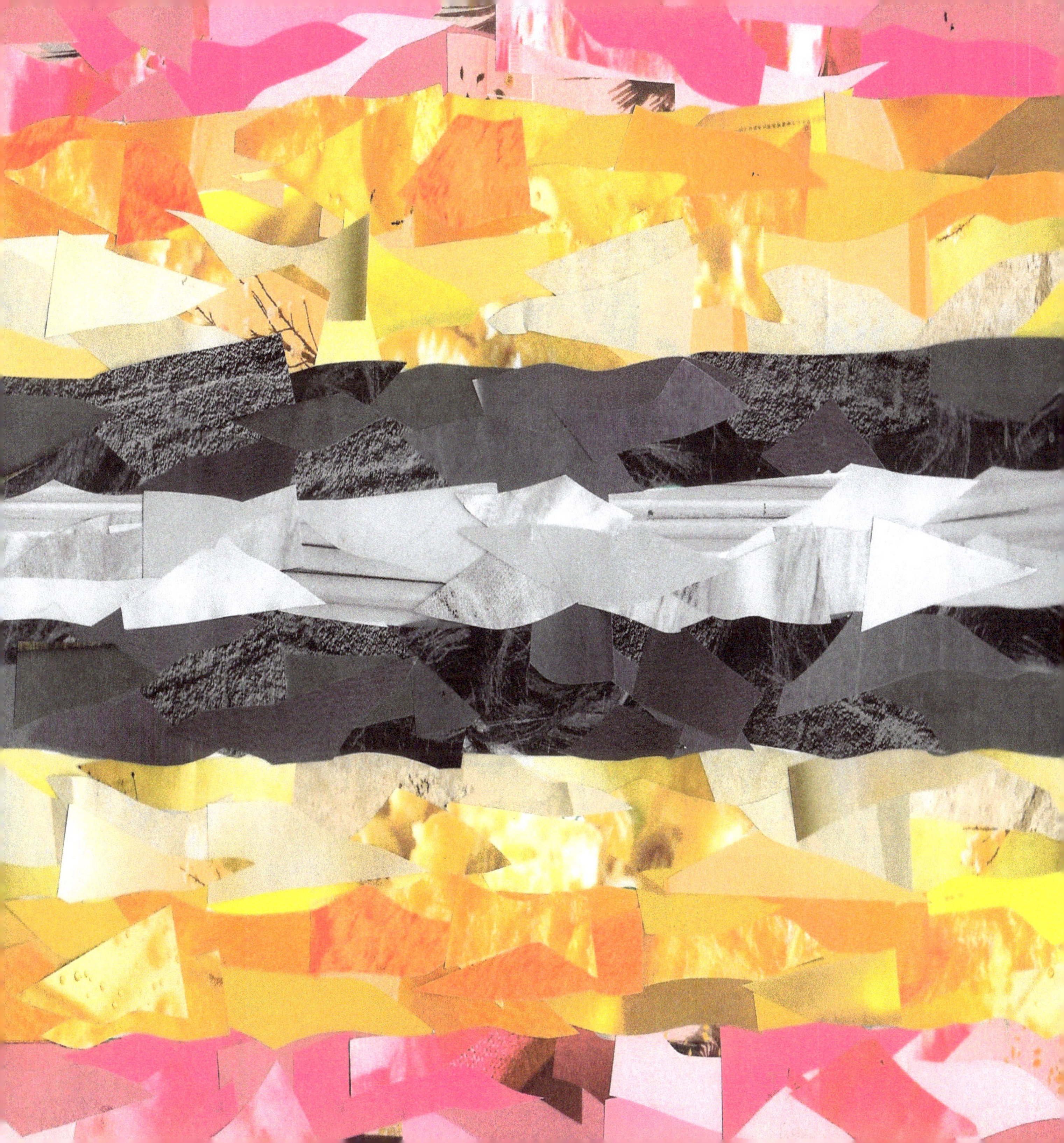

Chapter 5

Subcultures and More within the LGBT+ Community

A number of subcultures and different relationship types have developed in the LGBT+ community over the years as the community has grown and more people have found others like them. This section only mentions a handful of these relationships and subcultures and is by no means approaching the broad definitions and scope that the rest of this book discusses.

Being LGBT+ can look very different for a lot of people in practice, and often this can be in their relationships and general day to day life. It can also come across in the larger pockets of the LGBT+ community where there is a broader spectrum of experiences of one identity, like gay.

This is just mean to give you a small idea of what exists out there, and hopefully spurs you to look for your own subcultures if that is something that interests you.

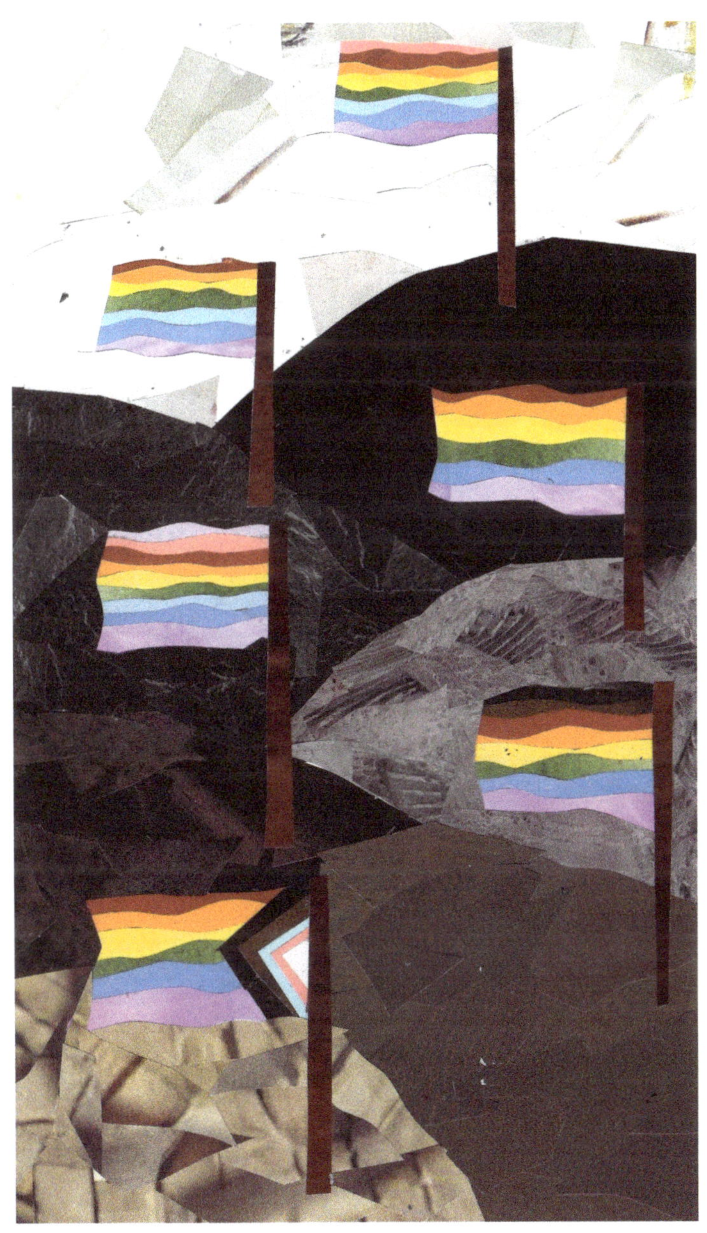

Bears

Bears are a subculture within the gay community. Bears are typically larger, harrier, and more masculine men within the gay, male community.[9] Originally, this was usually used for harrier, masculine gay men. However, it has become more specific over time as other subcommunities has developed while the LGBT+ community has experienced more public growth since being not straight has become more accepted by the general public.

It is important to note that this term is often used by any man attracted to other man so it will include bisexual men and other men that experience some form of multigender attraction. This subculture has spurred more than social circles of similar people, it has also inspired the creation of media like BEAR Magazine which is dedicated to Bears.

The Bear pride flag has seven stripes of dark brown, orange, yellow, a light yellow, white, grey, and black. Not shown in this interpretation is that a bear pawprint that is usually shown in the upper left-hand corner of most Bear pride flags.

Well Known Fictional Bears: The comic AJ and Magnus about a boy and his dog who has gay parents. One of them, John Parker, is a bear.

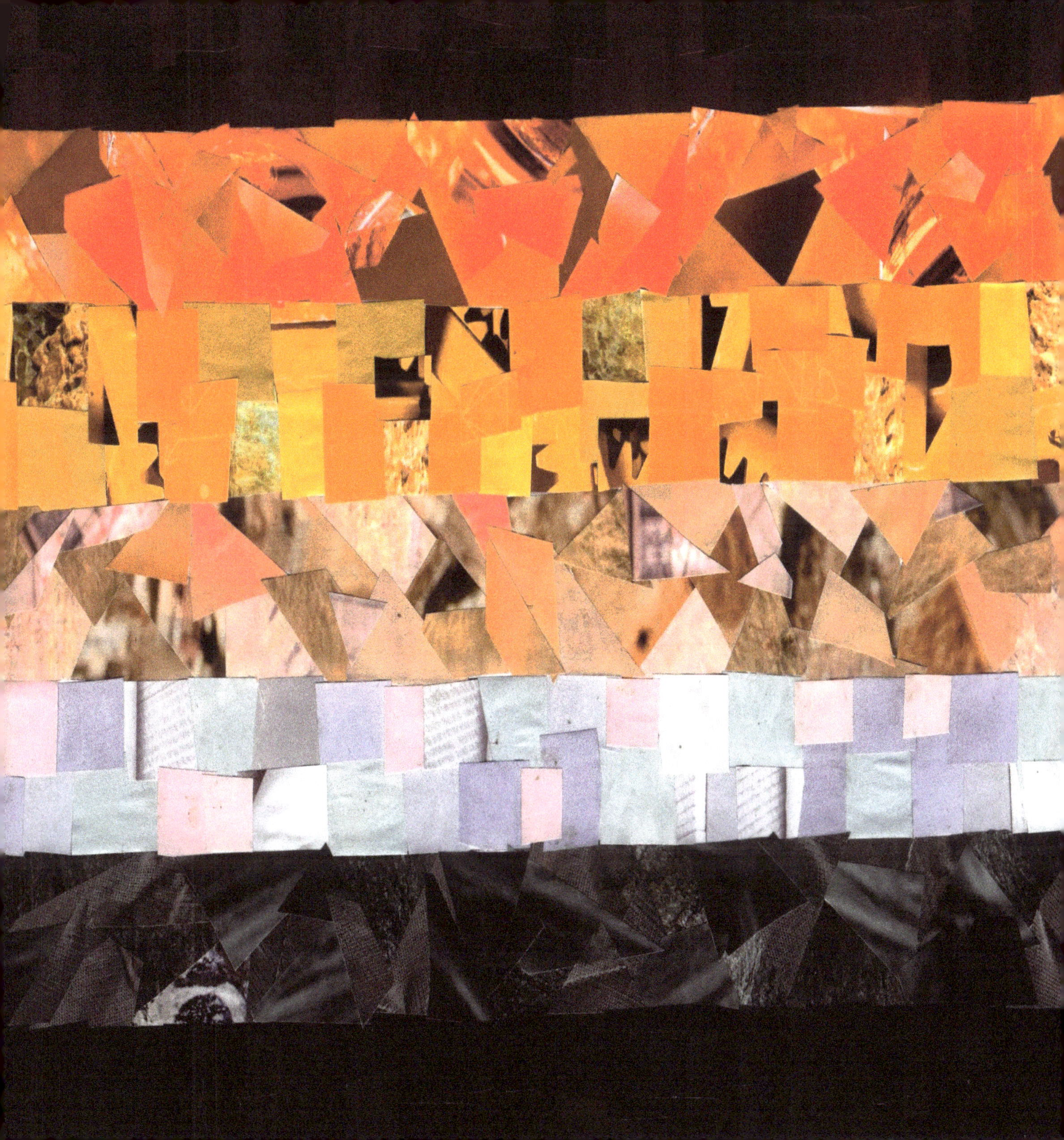

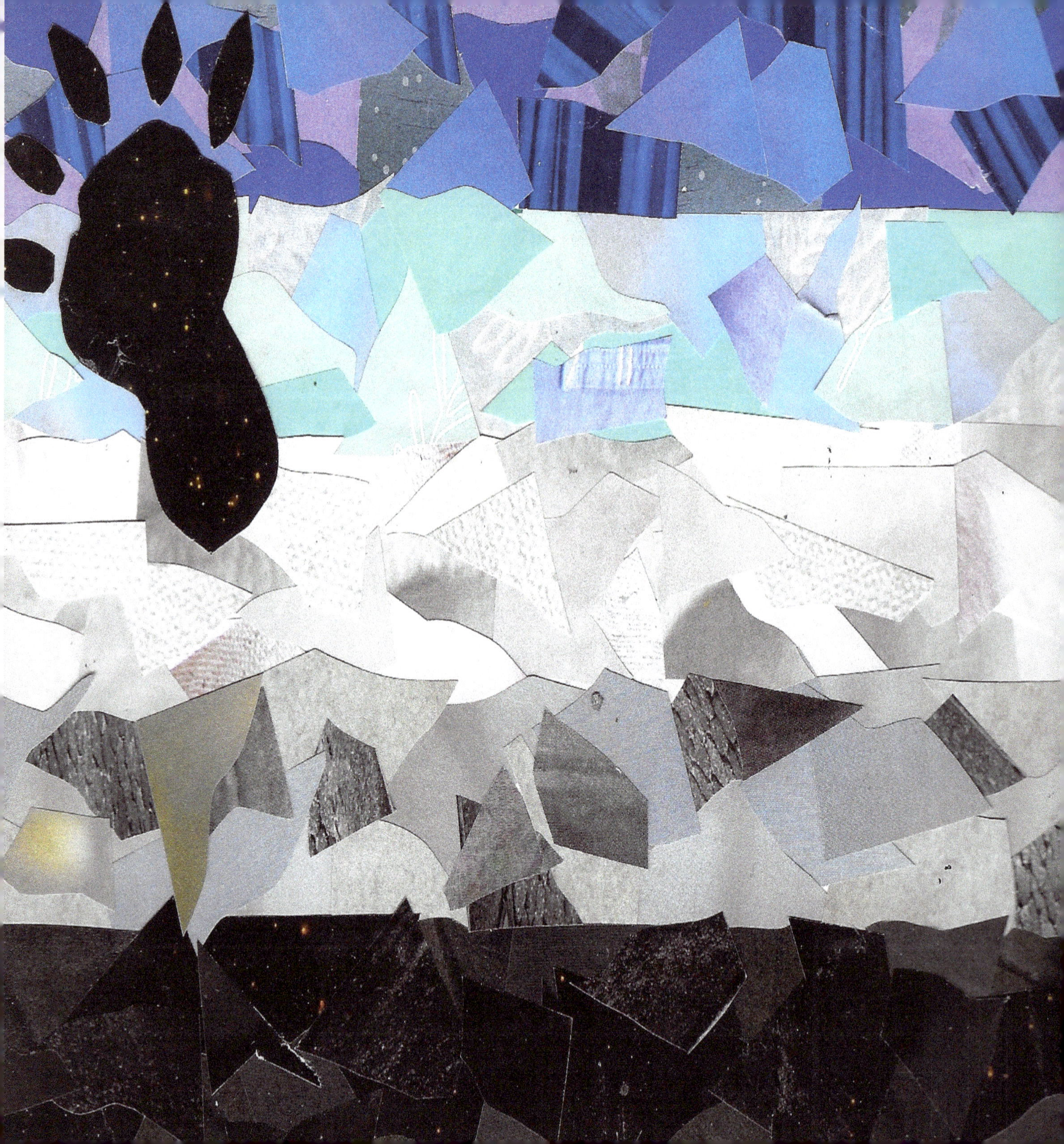

Otter

Much like a Bear, an Otter is another subculture within the gay community, specifically of men attracted to other men. An Otter tends to be slimmer than a bear but is a hairy man.

It is important to note that, much like in the Bear community, this term is often used by any man attracted to other man so it will include bisexual men and other men that experience some form of multigender attraction.

The Otter pride flag has five stripes of dark blue, light blue, white, grey, and black. In the upper left hand corner is a black otter pawprint.

Leathers

Though not directly part of the LGBT+ community for everyone involved, the Leathers community has been closely linked with LGBT+ people for decades. This community is noted by practices of and styles of dress organized around sexual activities that involve leather garments. This is partially because for the longest time, both the LGBT+ community and Leathers were wrongly thought of as sexually deviant.

A lot of this culture stemmed for the 1940s after World War II and has grown into a much larger community since then.[10] Since then, they have participated in helping protect the LGBT+ community, especially during the AIDS crisis. Women who were part of the Leather community in particular were important in taking care of LGBT+ men who were most likely to contract AIDS and die without support of anyone else.

Thus, people who are part of the Leathers community may not be LGBT+ though many are, but they have continued to be part of Pride celebrations and allies to the community.

The Leathers pride flag is made up of nine stripes of black, blue, black, blue, white, blue, black, blue, and black. It has a red heart in the top left corner.

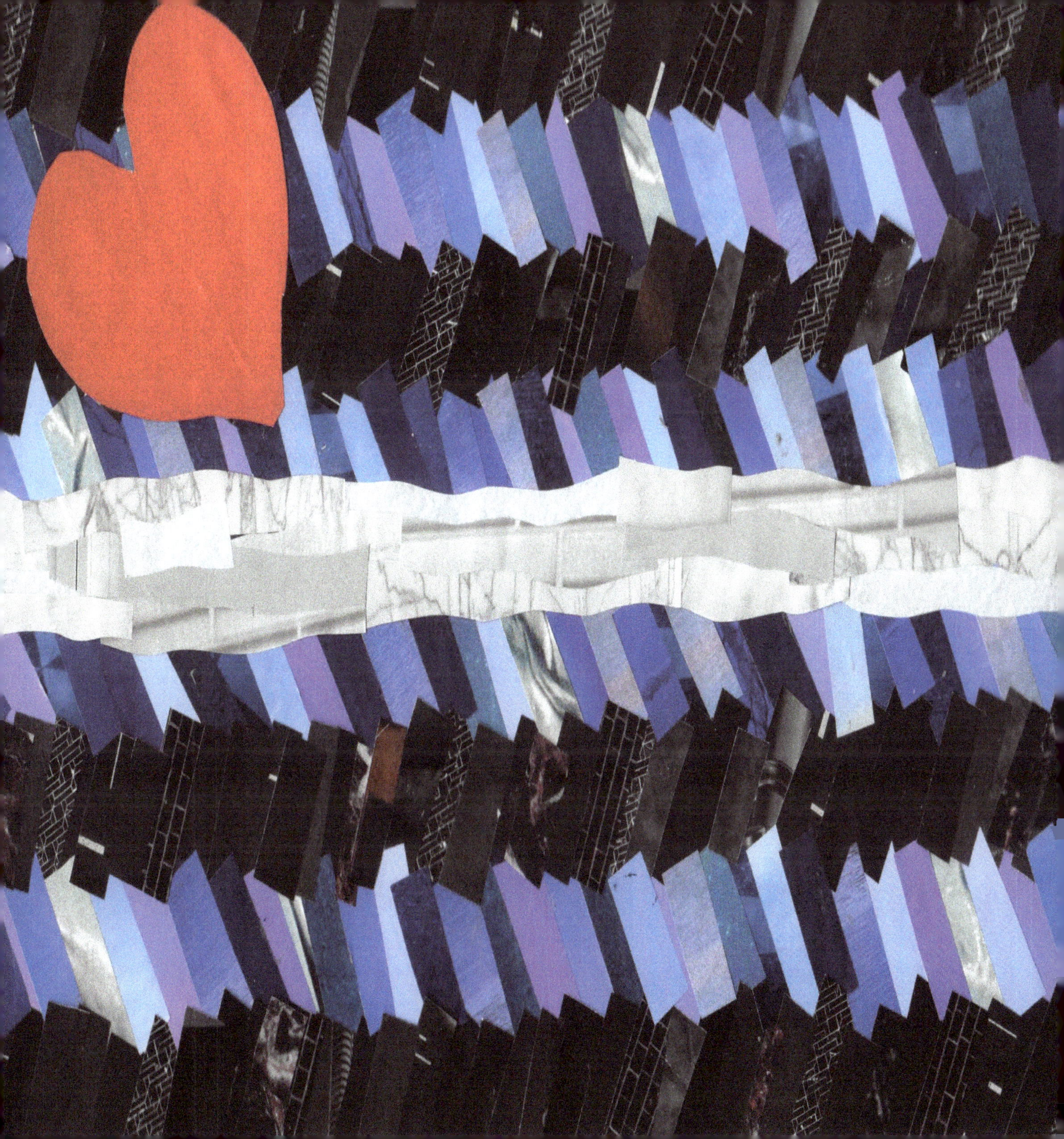

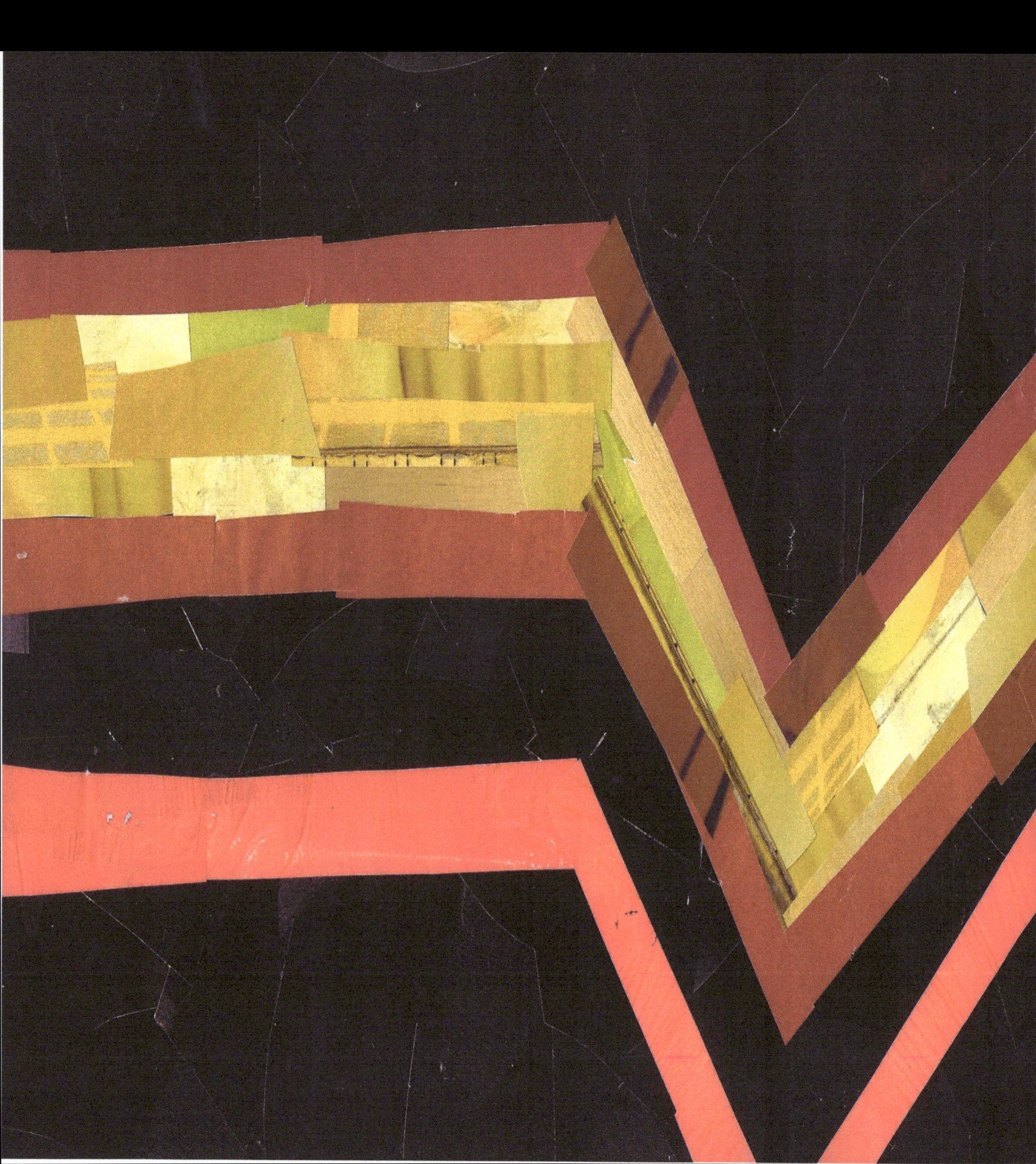

Rubber

The Rubber community is another community adjacent to the queer community like the Leather community. This pride flag is over twenty-five years old, making it one of the oldest known pride flags.

This pride flag is for people who are part of the rubber and latex kink community. It's often seen at pride parades and the community has a large number of LGBT+ members, though not all within it are queer themselves. Still, given the fact that people within kink communities like the Rubber community are often marginalized or pushed aside if their interests are known, the Rubber community is often seen in Pride parades and as allies of the LGBT+ community when they are not part of the community through some other identity.

Thus, people who are part of the Rubber community may not be LGBT+ though many are, but they have continued to be part of Pride celebrations and allies to the community.

The pride flag is a bit different as it is not the traditional straight lines of other pride flags. The background in black with one large yellow strip outline by red that creates a V on the right side. This is mirrored by a smaller red stripe underneath it.

Polyamorous

Polyamorous people are part of the LGBT+ community, and they tend to have a bit different looking relationships than the ones society is used to seeing. Polyamorous people will have intimate relationships with more than one person. These are done with informed consent of everyone involved.

The relationships in a polyamorous relationship may look different between each set of people within the relationship. Not everyone will have the same connection with everyone within the group and some may be open relationships rather than a set group of people.

The important part of polyamorous relationships is that they are heavily reliant on communication. This is because these relationships do involve more than two people and require trust and ongoing informed consent.

The older polyamorous flag, pictured below, has three stripes of blue, red, and black. There is the pi symbol in the middle of the red stripe in yellow. The updated polyamorous pride flag has a white triangle on the left with tip going between the first and second stripes. There is a sideways, yellow heart inside the triangle. The three stripes on the flag are blue, pink, and purple.

Well Known Polyamorous Relationship: William Moulton Marston (the writer of Wonder Woman), Elizabeth Holloway Marston, and Olive Byrne lived together for years and were polyamorous.

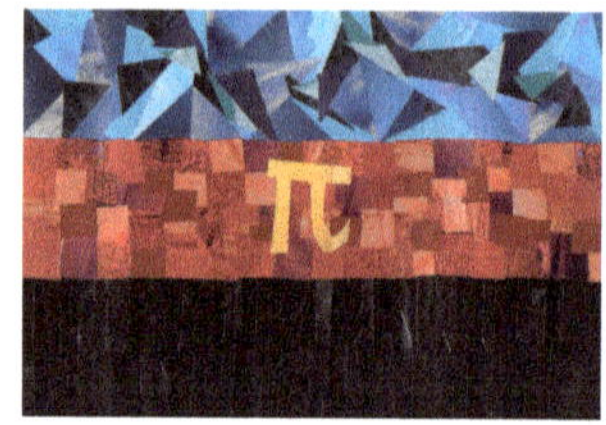

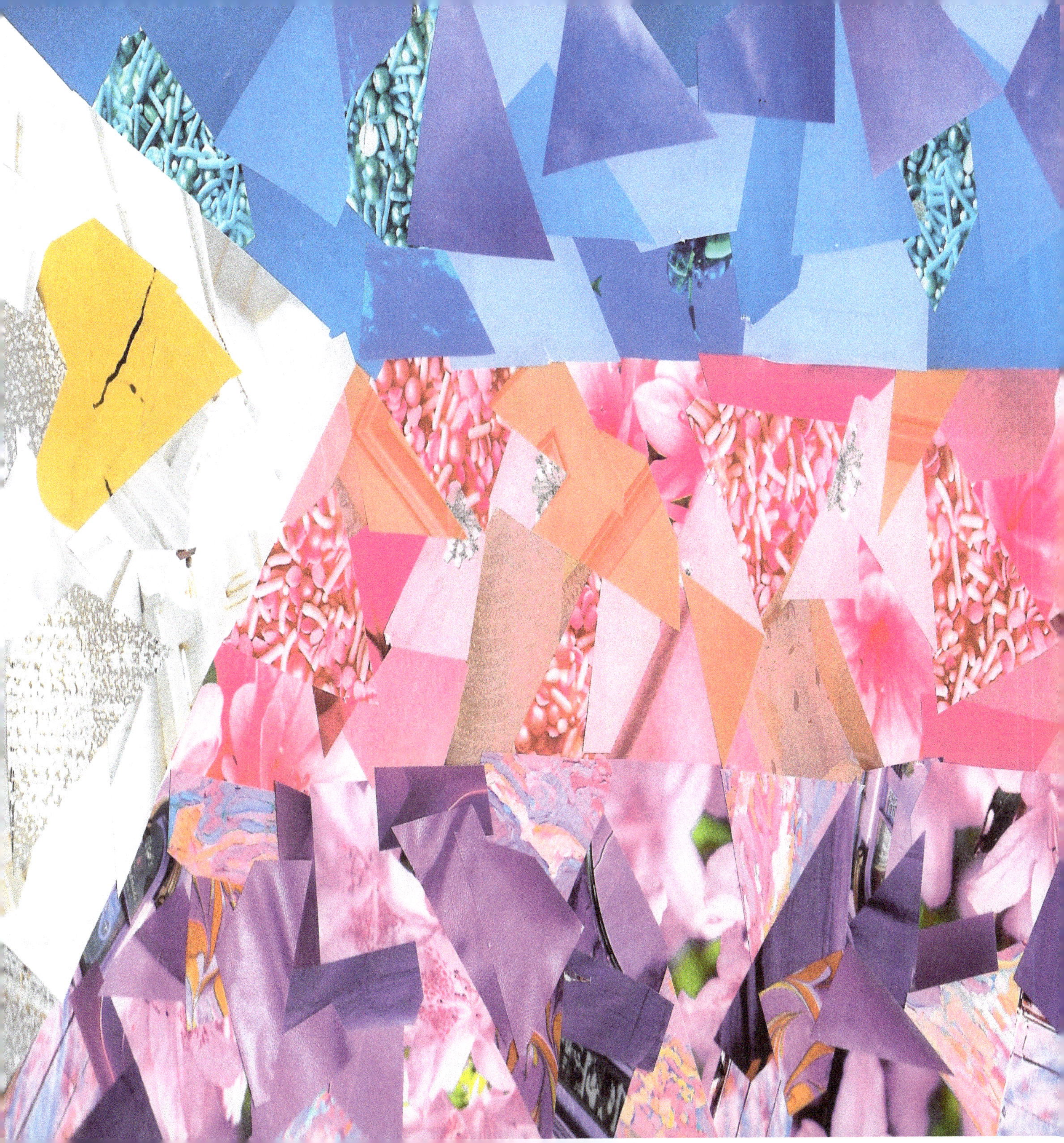

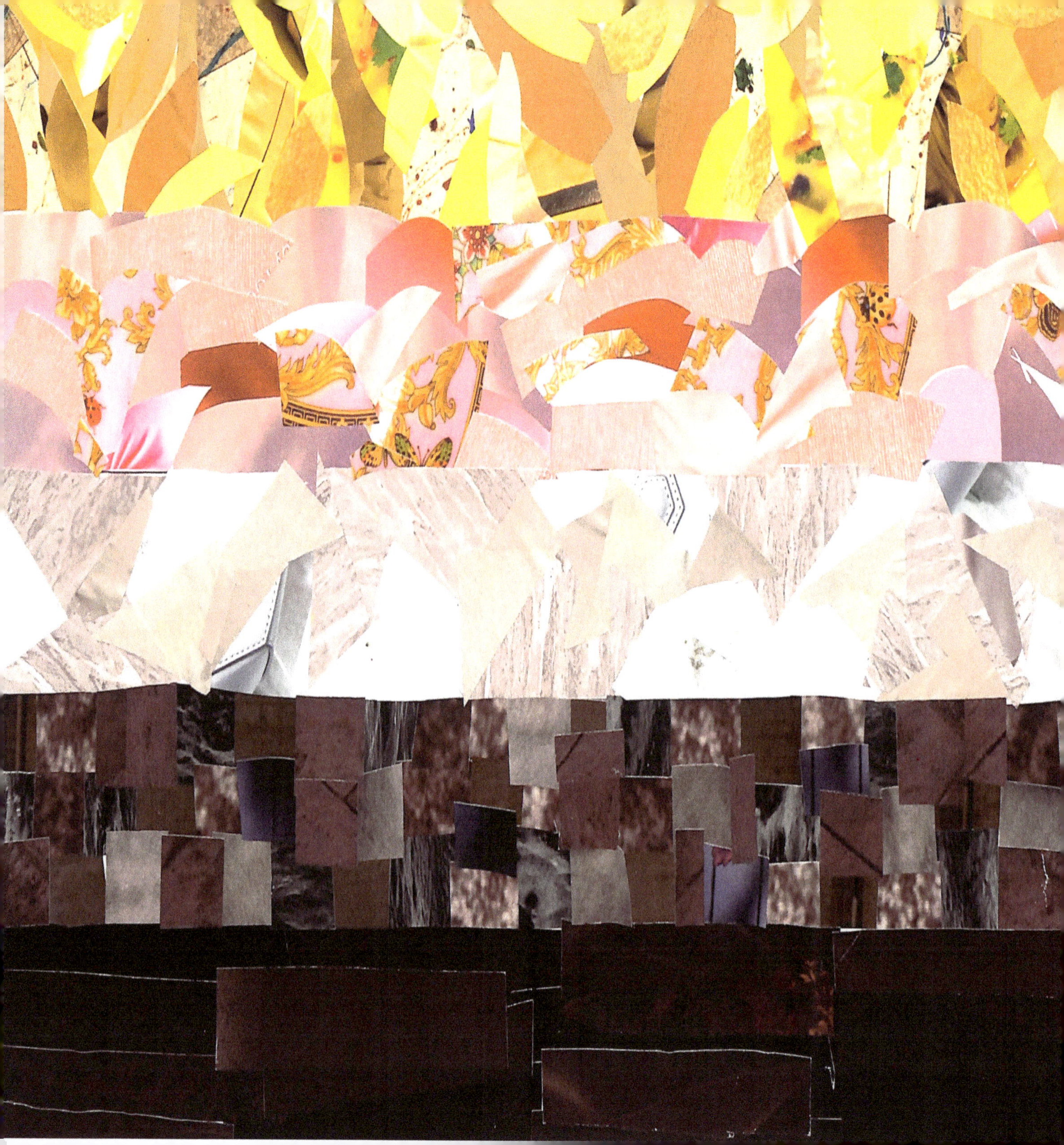

Queerplatonic Relationships

Queerplatonic relationships (QPRs) can be a formed through an intense bond that is not romantic between two people. It is generally platonic but far more intense than many people would associate with a platonic relationship as the people generally live together long term and provide far more emotional support than one would find in the average friendship.

QPRs can be formed regardless of how someone identifies sexually or romantically. They also may involve more than two people, so a person may have multiple queerplatonic partners.

People who want to enter these kinds of relationship may experience squishes, or the platonic version of a crush. Again, these are more intense than the average wish to be someone's friend as they tend to want to have a far more intense platonic relationship with someone.

The Queer Platonic Relationship flag is five stripes of yellow, pink, white, grey, and black.

Voidpunk

Voidpunk is a subculture within the LGBT+ community for people who feel disconnected or rejected from humanity.

People on the aromantic and asexual spectrums are often the ones drawn to this community, though many neurodivergent people, disabled people, nonbinary people, people of color, and others who are frequently dehumanized by society can be drawn to the voidpunk community as well.

The voidpunk community is based on embracing ideas of not being human.

The voidpunk pride flag is made up of five lines, four of the same size and a thin white line in the middle. In the middle of the thin white line is a black circle. Two stripes on top of it are dark purple and light purple. The two stripes below the white line are light green then dark green.

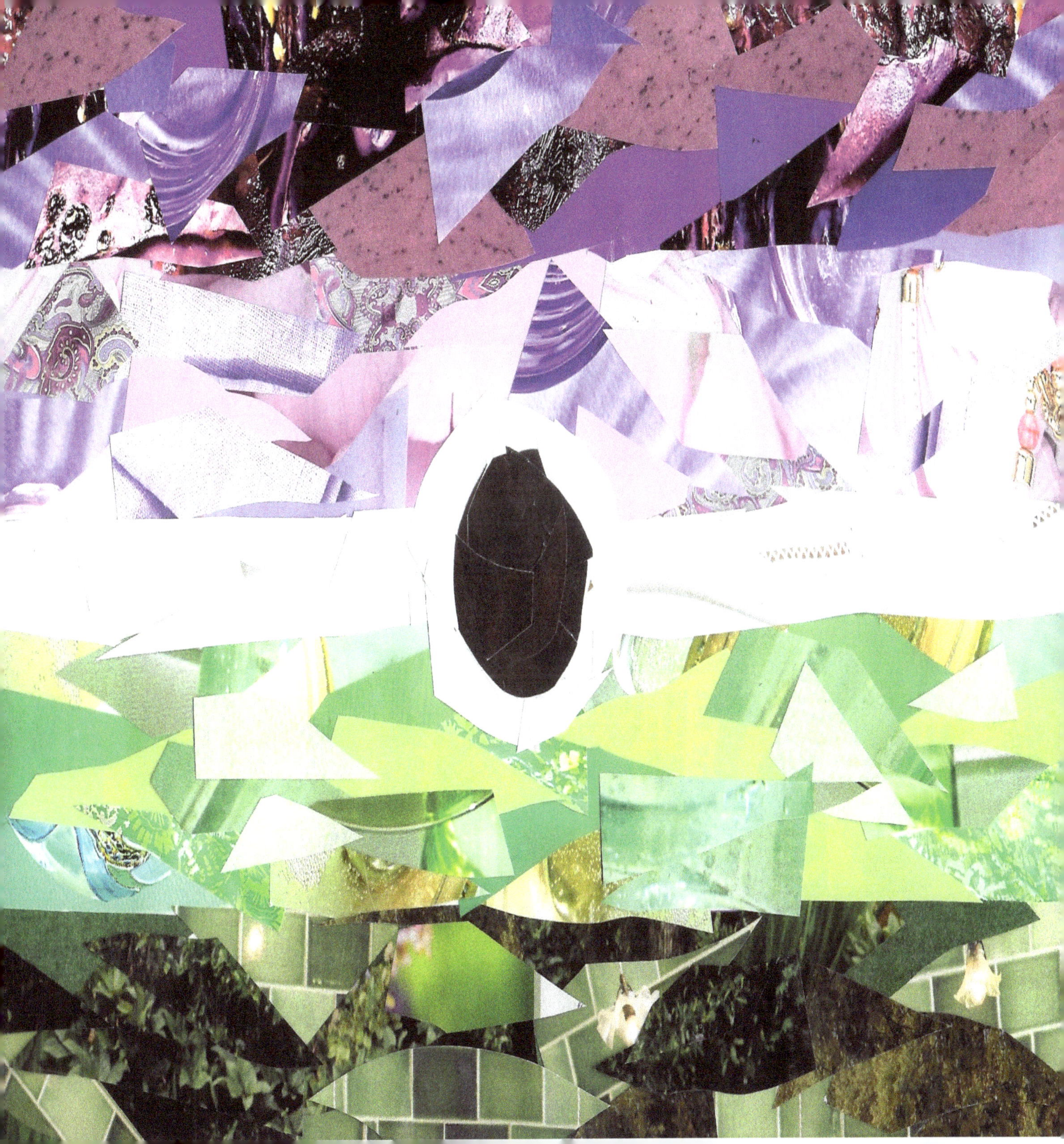

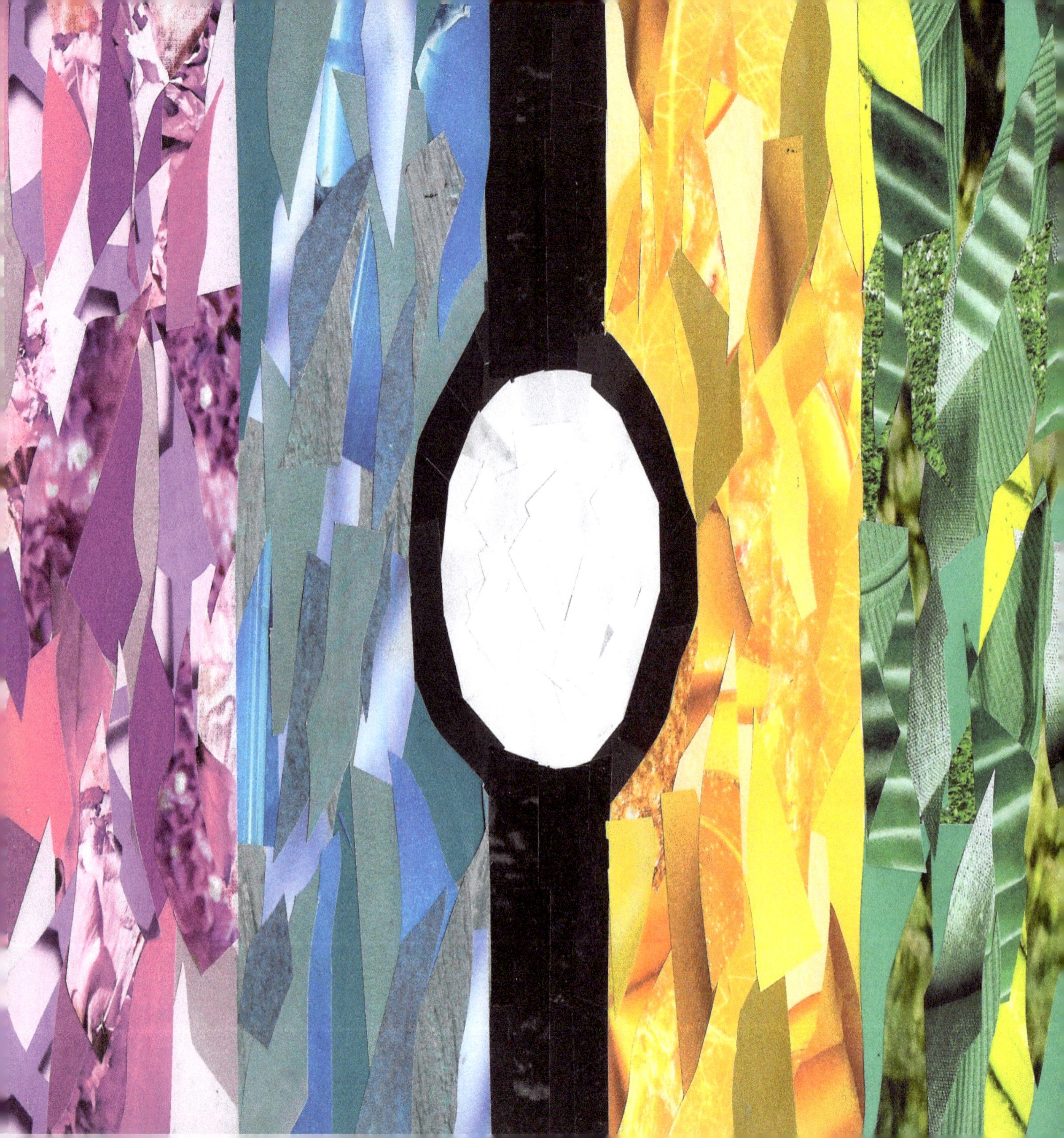

Lovepunk

Lovepunk is both an identity and an opposition to the societal ideas around love. Thus, sometimes it is a subculture, which is why it's been placed in this section.

People who are lovepunk reject norms of all kinds including: gender, attraction, orientation, and relationships. They also resist aphobia, or prejudice against asexual, aromantic, and aplatonic people and their communities. A lovepunk person doesn't have to be aromantic, asexual, or aplatonic, but they do stand with those communities.

Being lovepunk is open to anyone who wants to defy societal norms around love. That can be an active choice or just the way one exists day to day, and both are just as lovepunk as the other.

The lovepunk flag has five vertical stripes, four of equal width and one thin black strip in the middle with a white circle in the center of it. On the left, the stripes are purple and blue. On the right, the stripes are yellow and green.

Gender Nonconforming

Gender nonconforming people are people who have behavior or gender expression that does not match masculine or feminine gender norms. People who are gender nonconforming can be transgender, nonbinary, and even cisgender as it is merely a matter of a person's gender expression, not their identity.

Importantly, this does not necessarily make a person part of the LGBT+ community, though they may face similar issues to people who are not cisgender. A straight, cisgender man with painted nails or who likes to wear dresses and skirts could be gender nonconforming because he is not doing what society expects of masculine people. The same could be said of a straight, cisgender woman who wears men's suits and has short hair.

The gender nonconforming flag has seven stripes. Two thick, purple stripes are on the outside. In between the two purple stripes are five stripes that are light purple, blue, white, blue, and light purple.

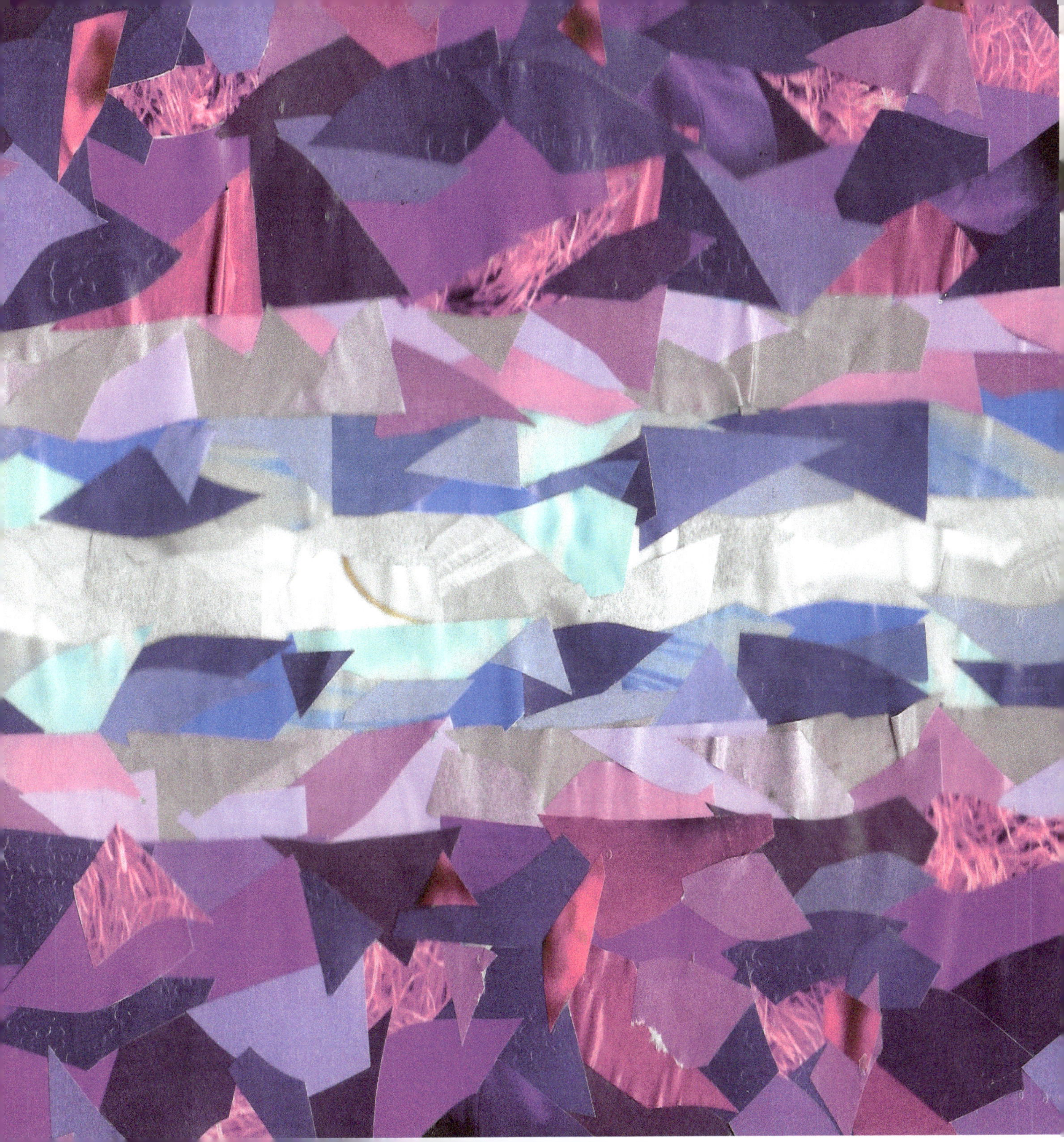

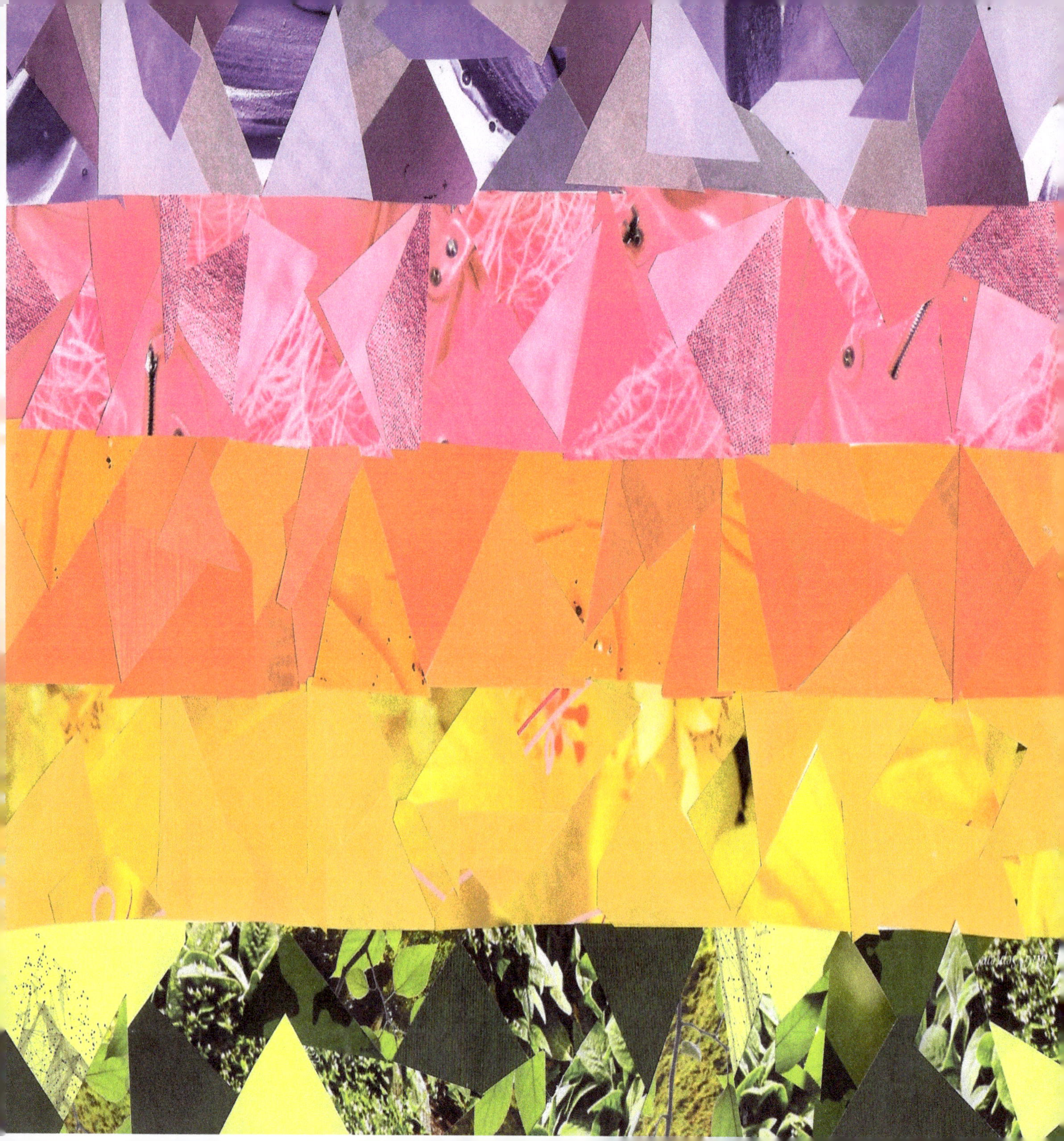

Amatopunk

Amatopunk people fight the idea that romantic relationships are necessary and that love must be done in a certain way. This includes fighting against the idea that everyone must experience a certain kind of love.

Overall, amatopunk actively push back against society's amatonormativity. Amatonormativity is the assumption within society that everyone must pursue or want to pursue a romantic, monogamous relationship. This view leaves almost no room for asexual, aromantic, polyamorous, and others outside of the traditional view of a relationship to exist without judgement or rejection in society unless they force themselves to fit the 'right' idea of what society expects of people.

The amatopunk pride flag has five equal sized stripes. The stripes are purple, pink, orange, yellow, and green.

Drag

Drag is when a person dresses up and exaggerates their features to perform as a certain gender on stage, usually to music.

People are most familiar with drag queens. Drag queens are usually men who dress up as women to perform and lip-sync. Though many people are more aware of drag queens, drag kings are also part of this community. Drag kings dress and perform as men alongside or independent of drag queens, and both may appear at a drag show. Importantly, a person's gender identity does not dictate if they are a drag king or queen, a woman can be a drag queen and a man can be a drag queen. There are also people who dress androgynously to do drag.

Often, drag kings and queens will adopt a stage name to go with their new onstage personas. These can be puns around the music they use or new names to go with their shows.

People who do drag have long been intertwined with the LGBT+ community, whether the person is LGBT+ or not. They've brought visibility to issues, participated in activism, and been part of pride for decades. On top of this, people who do drag often are targeted the same way in legislation and protests as the LGBT+ community is.

The drag pride flag has three stripes with a pink crown in the center stripe surrounded by stars. (The stars are not pictured in this rendition). The purple stripe is for the passion a person has for drag. The white stripe is for the blank slate a person's body and face are for new characters to create. The blue stripe is for self-expression and loyalty. The crown in the middle of the white stripe stands for leadership. The stars around it signify the many forms of drag.

Well Known People Who Did/Do Drag: Marsha P. Johnson (part of the Stonewall Riots), Ru Paul (TV host), and Vico Ortiz (actor).

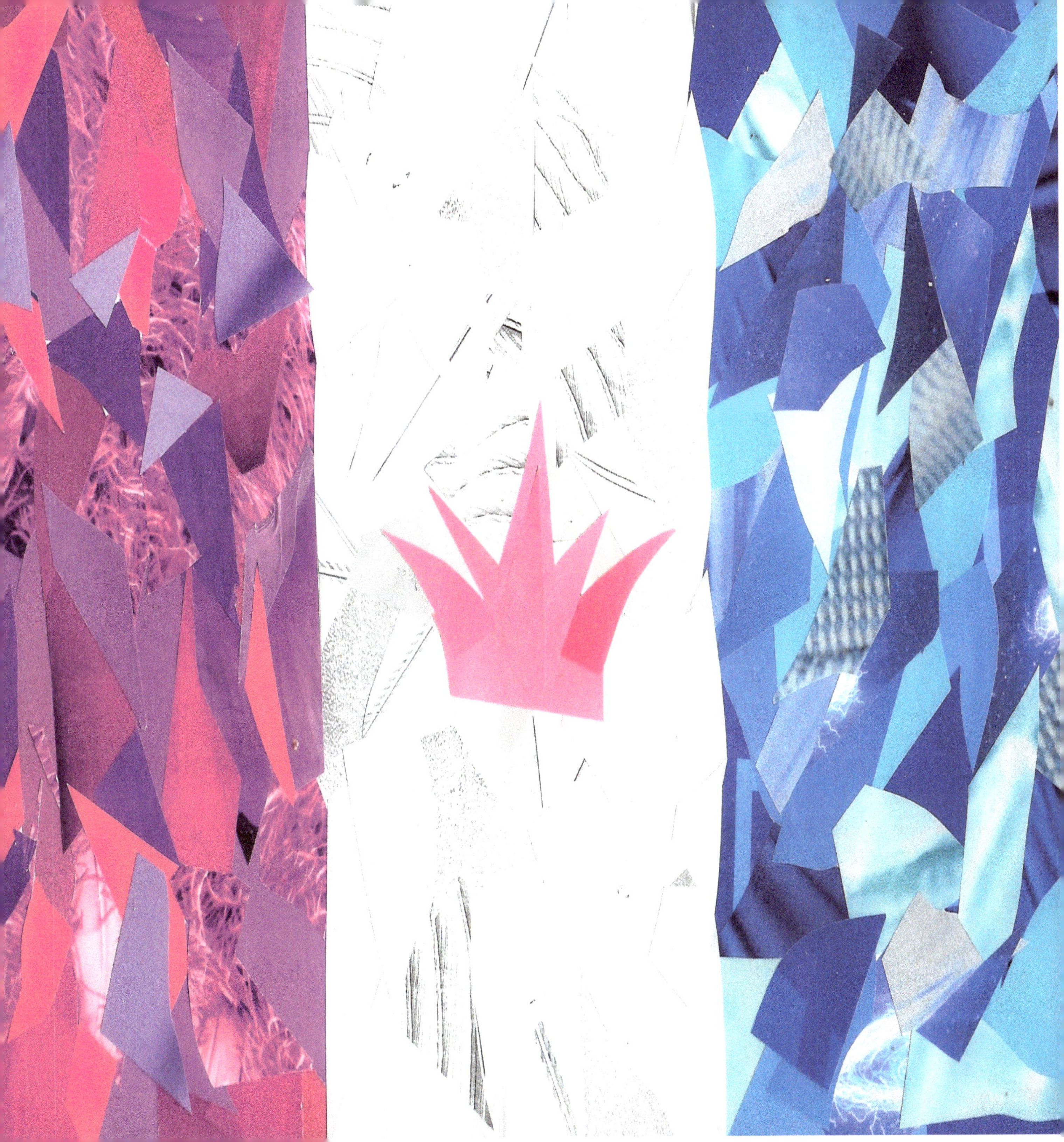

So what about Allies?

Allies are not part of the LGBT+ community. They are friends of the community and people that will stick up for their LGBT+ friends and others. However, they are not part of the community and will not be.

These are people that actively support the community, and that is greatly appreciated. This a term that others can likely give to heteroromantic, heterosexual, cisgender friends, or people that they feel are doing the work to make our world more accepting.

Sometimes, people who are still in the closet or questioning will use Ally as a term to go to LGBT+ events without outing themselves. Those people are or may be part of the LGBT+ community, but that is a different situation. As no one is required to come out, these people are no less welcome in our community.

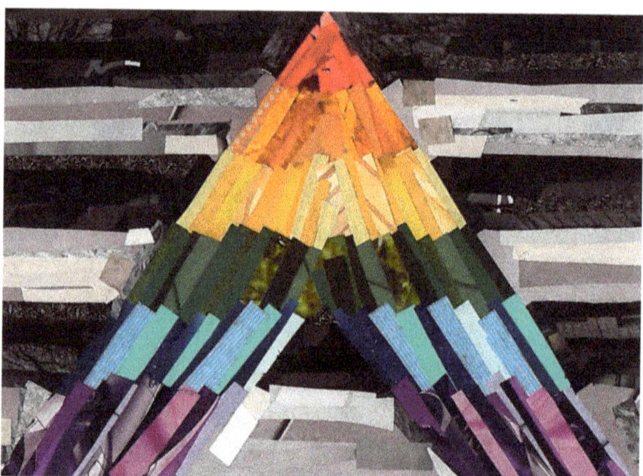

Thus, no A in the acronym stands for Ally.

Acknowledgements and How This Book Came to Be

This book was originally start as a series of pride flags in 2017 and has continued to grow since then. The first flag was the asexual flag, my own flag, at the end of pride month in 2017 on June 27, 2017. Since then, I continued to make pride flags off and on in my collages as a color study and a fun way to represent the community I have continued to find myself a part of.

The writing itself stemmed from the art project over a number of years after I had created many pride flags.

The pride flag collection will likely continue to grow as more identities are named and I continue to learn. I hope you enjoy the book and the artwork that comes with it. It has been many years in the making.

Looking for representation, I spent quite a bit of time researching people for identities to show some people who have been successful. I know that representation is often lacking in media, so I hope these people provide you some joy in seeing what LGBT+ people who you may or may not have heard of before. In some places where I was not able to find a real person, I put in fictional characters instead who identify as these labels. In the labels for people who experience multigender attraction or those on the aromantic or asexual spectrums, representation is more likely to be found in the broader or more well known terms. People may actually identify using more niche terms that they do not talk about in public as much.

Since many of the identities in this book are what could be considered a micro label, there very well could be famous people out there that do not wish to expose that much of their identity to the general public and may use one of the umbrella terms that their label falls under. Plenty of LGBT+ people do this as they do not want to give a whole vocabulary lesson every time they come out. However, you identify and whichever label you prefer, know that you are not alone. Online communities are vibrant today, and there are at a minimum thousands and thousands of other people just like you.

There are likely a number of identities not listed here. New labels are being recognized regularly and terminology can change very quickly. If you have not found one that you find comfort and recognition in, that doesn't mean it isn't out there.

To the people that have taken the time to educate me, to suggest pride flags, to inform me of updates, to ask if I had done a certain flag, thank you. This book wouldn't have as many pride flags without you, and I love learning more about those identities.

To my mother, who proofread this book as a person who knew little of what I was writing, thank you for taking that time (and for catching a few spelling errors).

To Pieter Favier, the professor that taught my 2-D design class, thank you introducing me to collage making in 2016.

And to my friends, namely Grace, Rebecca, Lional, and Sean, thank you for always being supportive of my art and encouraging me to do what I love.

Finally, to my Tumblr followers, who have been here for it all, thank you. I've grown social media presence on a number of platforms, but Tumblr has always had a special place in my heart for being where I started, and you have seen it all in a way that most others haven't.

For any mistakes I made, I apologize. I did my best to make my language inclusive and my definitions accurate and open ended as identity is so incredibly nuanced from person to person. Much of this is the culmination of years of research from making the pride flags themselves and I did my best to represent those that I do know of well. I will continue to work towards positive and inclusive language around the LGBT+ community and in general.

Wishing you lots of Pride,

Jennifer

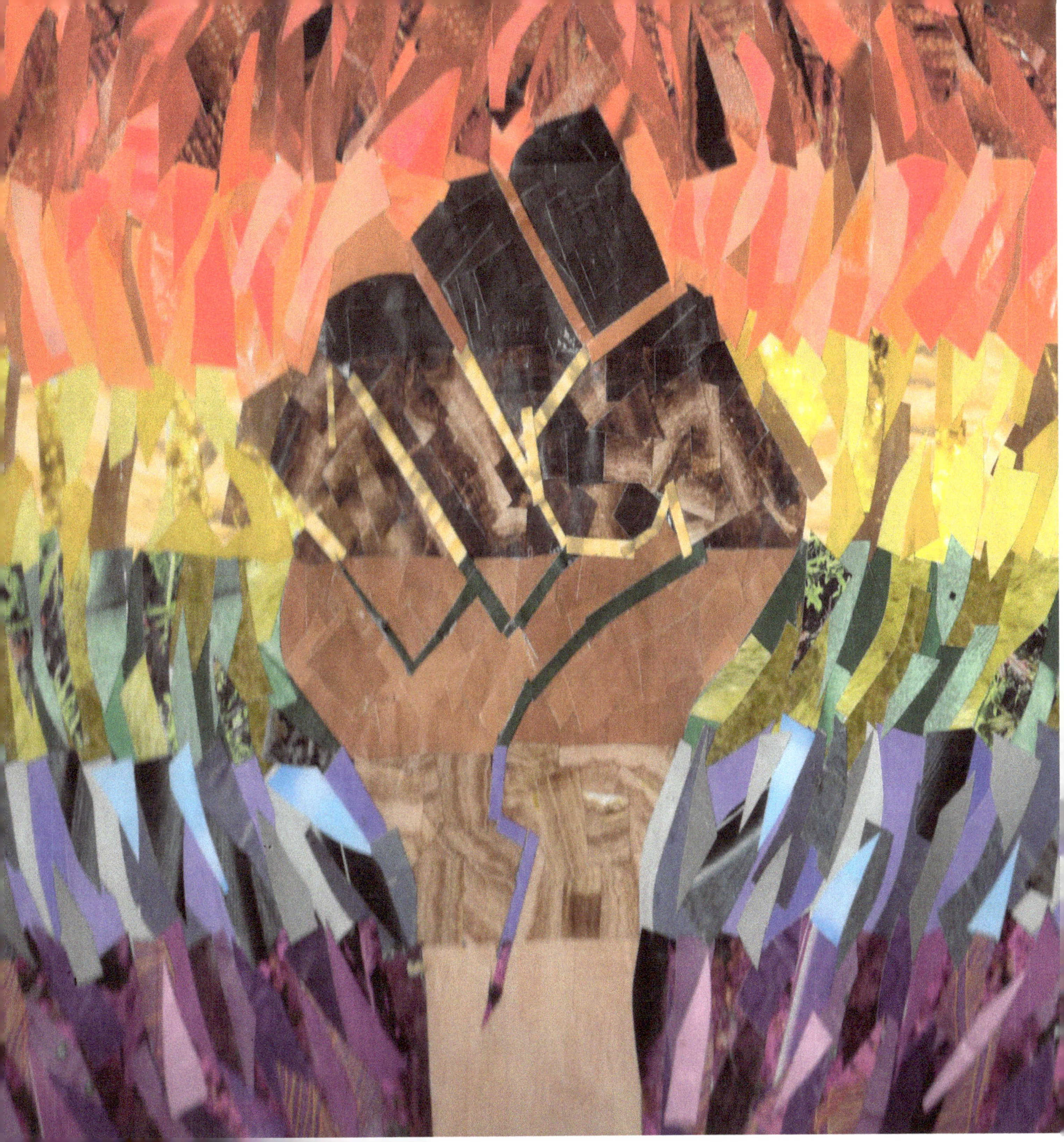

Citations for Prior Works

Page 2: Frederick, J. (2021, December). Gilbert Baker Pride Flag. *Beyond Words Literary Magazine.*
Page 7: Frederick, J. (2020, October). Philadelphia Pride. *Witness* Volume XXXIII.
Page 11: Frederick, J. (2023, June). Explosion of Pride. Hung in Baltimore City Hall for several months.

References

[1] Jeffrey Jones, "LGBT Identification Rises to 5.6% in Latest U.S. Estimate," *Gallup*, 24 February 2021, https://news.gallup.com/poll/329708/lgbt-identification-rises-latest-estimate.aspx

[2] "What's Intersex?," *Planned Parenthood*, https://www.plannedparenthood.org/learn/gender-identity/sex-gender-identity/whats-intersex

[3] Written by Rachel Alatalo in 2017 and Edited by Matthew Solomon in 2021,"Flags of the LGBTIQ Community," *OutRight Action International*, 20 September 2021, https://outrightinternational.org/content/flags-lgbtiq-community

[4] Victor Salvo, "Two Spirit People," *The Legacy Project*, https://legacyprojectchicago.org/milestone/two-spirit-people

[5]Lily Puckett, "Merriam-Webster Just Added 2 Very Important, Inclusive Words to the Dictionary," *Teen Vogue*, 22 April 2016, https://www.teenvogue.com/story/merriam-webster-cisgender-genderqueer-added-to-dictionary

[6] "Neutrois," *Neutrois.Com*, http://neutrois.com/

[7] Moyer, Paul B. (2015). The Public Universal Friend: Jemima Wilkinson and Religious Enthusiasm in Revolutionary America. Cornell University Press. ISBN 978-0-8014-5413-4.

[8] Marlowelune. (2016, July 5). Non-binary Love: An update and a poll. Tumblr. Retrieved October 4, 2022, from https://marlowelune.tumblr.com/post/146953154069/non-binary-love-an-update-and-a-poll.

[9] Suresha, Ron (2009). "Bearness's Big Blank: Tracing the Genome of Ursomasculinity". Bears on Bears: Interviews and Discussions. Lethe Press. p. 83. ISBN 978-1590212448.

[10] "Elegy for the Valley of Kings," by Gayle Rubin, in In Changing Times: Gay Men and Lesbians Encounter HIV/AIDS, ed. Levine et al., University of Chicago Press.

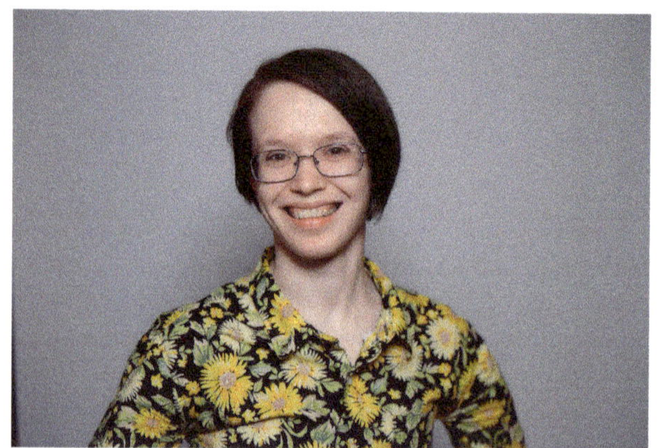

Jennifer Frederick is a lawyer, writer, and artist based out of Baltimore, Maryland. They started creating collages in 2016 after a 2-D design class in college and have been writing since a young age. Their artwork has been featured in a number of publications as well as a second place winner of Common Cause's My Voice, My Art, Our Cause Artivism Contest in 2021 and having their work on display for several months in Baltimore City Hall in 2023.

Find Jennifer and their work on social media: @lawofcollage on Tumblr, Instagram, and TikTok. Jennifer's Law of Collage on Facebook. (Formerly collagesofcollege, but that went away after graduating law school). Their shop can be found on Threadless at lawofcollage.threadless.com.

www.ingramcontent.com/pod-product-compliance
Ingram Content Group UK Ltd.
Pitfield, Milton Keynes, MK11 3LW, UK
UKHW061951290726
14090UKWH00021B/1177